TUTANKHAMUN

Nearly 100 years ago, English archaeologist Howard Carter and a team of dedicated Egyptologists and excavators discovered the well-preserved tomb of the pharaoh Tutankhamun in the Valley of the Kings, Egypt. The discovery surpassed the boundaries of archaeology and fired the imagination of people all over the world, profoundly influencing high, as well as popular culture and made millions of people aware of Ancient Egyptian civilisation. The Book of Tutankhamun will delve into the life, rule and influence of Ancient Egypt's most famous king, including how this advanced society functioned over 3000 years ago. It will also follow the journey of the team who researched Egyptian history, travelled through the vast valleys, dug through the desert sand and eventually unearthed the sacred tomb. Finally, it will list the trinkets, mementos and royal property found in the antechamber and annex, detail the recording and safeguarding process of these precious treasures and explore how the tomb's discovery remains significant to this day.

TUTANKHAMUN

Future PLC Richmond House, 33 Richmond Hill,
Bournemouth, Dorset, BH2 6EZ

Editorial
Author **Jaromir Malek**
Editor **Amy Best**
Designer **Madelene King**
Compiled by **Jacqueline Snowden & Laurie Newman**
Editorial Director **Jon White**
Senior Art Editor **Andy Downes**

Cover images
Getty Images

Photography
All copyrights and trademarks are recognised and respected

Advertising
Media packs are available on request
Commercial Director **Clare Dove**
clare.dove@futurenet.com

International
Head of Print Licensing **Rachel Shaw**
licensing@futurenet.com

Circulation
Head of Newstrade **Tim Mathers**

Production
Head of Production **Mark Constance**
Production Project Manager **Clare Scott**
Advertising Production Manager **Joanne Crosby**
Digital Editions Controller **Jason Hudson**
Production Managers **Keely Miller, Nola Cokely, Vivienne Calvert, Fran Twentyman**

Management
Chief Content Officer **Aaron Asadi**
Commercial Finance Director **Dan Jotcham**
Head of Art & Design **Greg Whitaker**

Printed by William Gibbons, 26 Planetary Road,
Willenhall, West Midlands, WV13 3XT

Distributed by Marketforce, 5 Churchill Place, Canary Wharf, London, E14 5HU
www.marketforce.co.uk Tel: 0203 787 9001

The content in this book was previously published in the Carlton book Tutankhamun: Egyptology's Greatest Discovery

All About History Tutankhamun Second Edition

CONTENTS

CHRONOLOGY OF THE EGYPTIAN NEW KINGDOM

1540–1069

All years are in BC and all dates are approximate

DYNASTY 18: 1540–1295

Ahmose (1540–1525; accession 1550)
Amenhotep I (1525–1504)
Thutmose I (1504–1492)
Thutmose II (1492–1479)
Hatshepsut, Queen (1479–1457)
Thutmose III (1479–1425)
Amenhotep II (1427–1401)
Thutmose IV (1401–1391)
Amenhotep III (1391–1353)
Amenhotep IV/Akhenaten (1353–1337)
Smenkhkare (1338–1336)
Tutankhaten/Tutankhamun (1336–1327)
Aye (1327–1323)
Haremhab (1323–1295)

DYNASTY 19: 1295–1186

Ramesses I (1295–1294)
Sety I (1294–1279)
Ramesses II (1279–1213)
Merneptah (1213–1203)
Amenmesse (1203–1200)
Sety II (1200–1194)
Siptah (1194–1186)
Twosre, Queen (1188–1186)

DYNASTY 20: 1186–1069

Setnakht (1186–1184)
Ramesses III (1184–1153)
Ramesses IV (1153–1147)
Ramesses V (1147–1143)
Ramesses VI (1143–1136)
Ramesses VII (1136–1129)
Ramesses VIII (1129–1126)
Ramesses IX (1126–1108)
Ramesses X (1108–1099)
Ramesses XI (1099–1069)

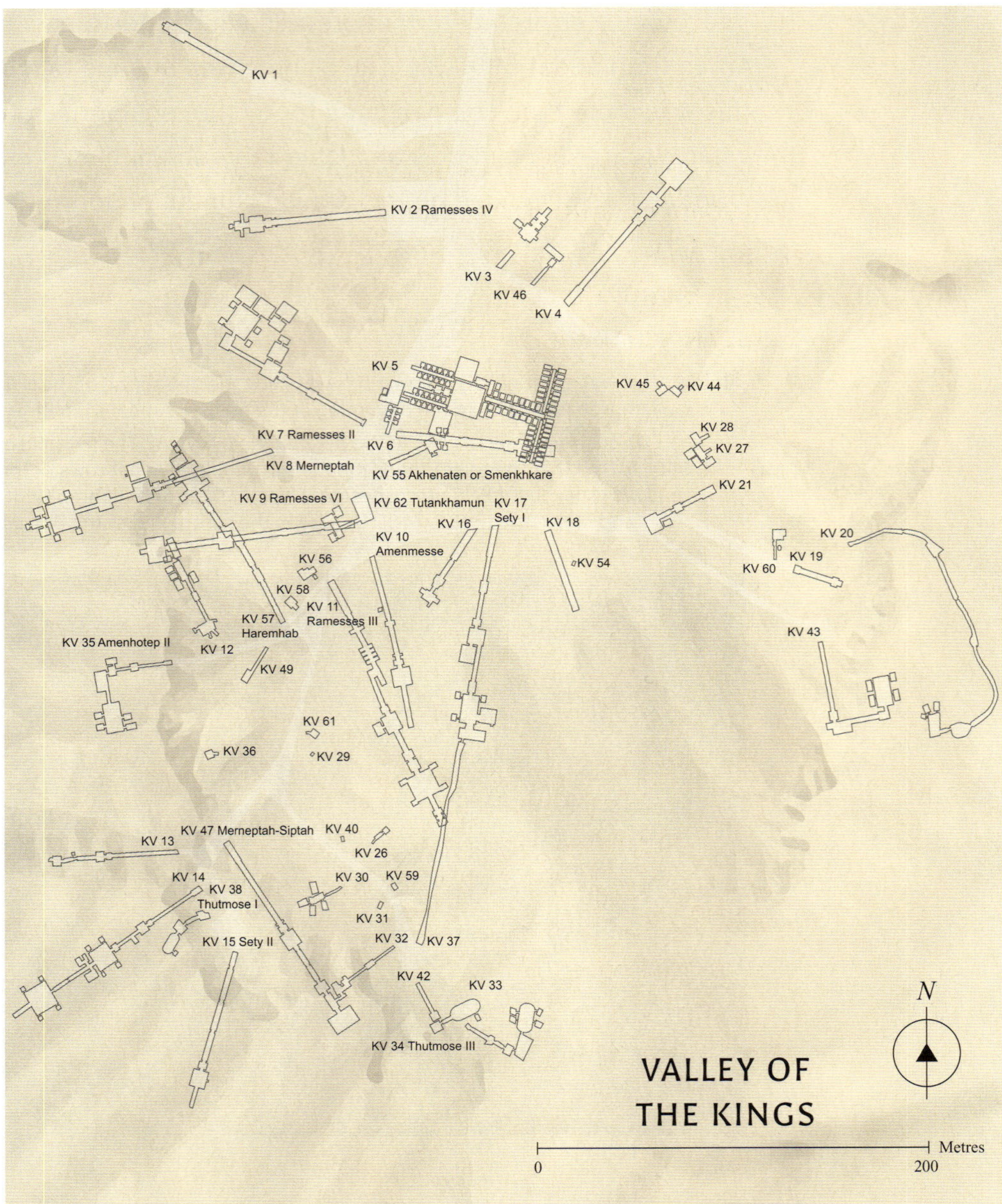

THE LAND AND PEOPLE OF ANCIENT EGYPT

Ancient Egyptian civilisation could not have existed without the exceptionally favourable environment that prevailed in the north-eastern corner of Africa from about 5000 BC. The climate was dry and rain infrequent, but this was more than compensated for by the regular rise of the river Nile, which occurred in mid-July and lasted through until September. Egyptian agriculture depended on this annual inundation for irrigation as well as for the fertile silt deposited on fields when the waters retreated.

Below: This wall painting is of two scribes watching the measuring of the crop, in the tomb of Menna. It probably dates to the beginning of the reign of Amenhotep III, around 1390 BC.

Opposite: An aerial view of the pyramid field of Giza. The pyramid of Khufu (2549–2526 BC) at the top of the picture is surrounded by neat rows of tombs of priests and officials, built to a uniform design. The pyramids of Khephren (2518–2493 BC) and Menkaure (2488–2460 BC) are in the centre and at the bottom left.

Many pyramids in Ancient Egypt were built as tombs for Pharaohs and to date there are over 130 that have been discovered

"The Black Land", as Egypt was called by its inhabitants, consisted of a narrow strip of enormously fertile ground on both banks of the river in the southern part of the country (Upper Egypt) and the broad Nile Delta which fans out as the Nile approaches the Mediterranean (Lower Egypt). The inhospitable neighbouring areas possessed valuable mineral resources and precious metal deposits, especially gold for which Egypt was famous. No other country in the area enjoyed such advantages and there was nobody to seriously challenge the Egyptian pharaohs' supremacy during the third millennium and much of the first half of the 2nd millennium BC. After about 1540 BC Egypt had to contend with other superpowers, initially the kingdom of Mitanni and then the Hittites, for the control of the Syro-Palestinian region, and eventually its own security.

The Egyptians were far from being one race. They were an amalgam of people living along the Nile who depended on the river for their subsistence and those who were driven from the areas further west by the progressive desiccation of the Sahara. There were also immigrants from north-western Asia. The Egyptian language is usually classified as Afro-Asiatic. It has connections with the languages of northern and eastern Africa as well as with the Semitic languages of western Asia.

Agriculture was by far the most important element of the economy in Egypt. Emmer and barley were the staple cereals, and various vegetables and fruit were also grown. The rearing of cattle was important and there were also extensive fowl-yards. The pharaoh was "the Lord of the Two Lands" (Upper and Lower Egypt), but land ownership was diverse. There were royal and temple estates and some that provided for the cult of the deceased and the needs of those employed in its maintenance. Some land was also awarded to officials and priests as payment in kind. This came with their positions and, in theory, they were entitled to it only during their lifetime. In practice, this was difficult to enforce and eventually led to private ownership of land.

Craftsmen who manufactured items of daily use, such as clothes, tools, pottery and furniture, were attached to royal, temple or funerary estates. The same was true of workshops that made tomb equipment. Workmen, craftsmen and artists engaged in the building of temples and the making of tombs were under direct royal or temple control; there were no independent builders or artists.

THE NILE INUNDATION

The dependence of Egypt's agriculture on the waters of the Nile was absolute. The Nile inundation arrived each year around 19 July (of the Julian calendar) and heralded the first day of the Egyptian calendar. Fields remained under water for the next three or four months. There were three seasons of four months each: akhet (inundation), peret (winter), and shemu (summer). A late arrival of the inundation, or an exceptionally high one, usually caused famine and destruction.

Above: The green and extremely fertile Nile Valley changes abruptly to the barren grey-yellow of the desert.

Opposite: Two men measuring the crop in the tomb of Menna, a "scribe of the fields of the Lord the Two Lands of Upper and Lower Egypt". This wall painting probably dates from the reign of Amenhotep III, around 1390 BC.

MINERALS, WOOD AND METALS

Ancient Egypt was rich in most of the minerals required by builders and sculptors, such as limestone, sandstone, granite, quartzite, basalt, alabaster and greywacke. Semi-precious stones, for example carnelian, jasper and feldspar, were also obtained locally. Obsidian was probably imported from Ethiopia and lapis lazuli from as far as Badakhshan in Afghanistan. Egypt lacked suitable timber for construction and shipbuilding purposes and had to import it from the Lebanon and Nubia. Copper came mostly from Sinai and the Nubian part of the Eastern Desert. Gold was mined in the Eastern Desert and Nubia. There were plentiful supplies of iron, although this did not become important until the middle of the 1st millennium BC.

SOCIETY, RELIGION AND ARTS

Although seemingly impervious to change, Egypt actually altered quite considerably in the course of nearly three millennia of pharaonic history. For much of this time there were only two significant groups in society: producers and high-level managers ("officials"). This situation changed in a radical way, however, during the New Kingdom, after about 1540 BC.

The largest social group consisted of peasants, who were attached to land from which they were not free to move. Their lives were entirely controlled by the landowner, who might be the state, a temple, a funerary estate or a wealthy official. Above this mass of producers there were local, low-level managers and scribes. Although their social status was no higher, they were materially better off.

The position of craftsmen who manufactured everyday goods, of workers in necropolis workshops, builders, artists and providers of services (domestic servants and also people employed in transport and limited internal commerce, etc) was similar. Their links to the institutions to which they were attached were unbreakable.

There was no significant equivalent to the "middle classes", although the number of independent farmers, initially very

small, was gradually increasing. There was no group whose position would correspond to that of slaves in classical antiquity. Captives were brought from military campaigns abroad and some were used as cheap labour for work in the harshest conditions, but these people represented only a fraction of the working population and the country's economic production certainly did not depend on them.

The privileged social group of managers consisted of government officials and senior administrators of royal estates in temple and necropolis management. The interconnections ensured that many held high priestly functions and also military ranks. Their livelihood came from the institutions to which they were attached, often in the form of land endowed with personnel that they then administered for themselves.

Opposite: A funeral procession depicted in the tomb of the High Priest of the God Ptah, Ptahemhet, at Saqqara during the reigns of Tutankhamun (1336–1327 BC) or Aye (1327–1323 BC).

Above, left: A typical way of portraying human figures, from the tomb of the vizier Ramose at Thebes during the reign of Amenhotep III (1391–1353 BC).

Above, right: A granodiorite statue of the Mayor of the City of Thebes, Sennufer, his wife Sentnay and their daughter Mutnofret, from the reign of Amenhotep II (1427–1401 BC).

During the New Kingdom (after 1540 BC) the priesthood became a third separate social group. Previously, priestly offices were held by officials of local and royal administration and priests of the lowest ranks were little more than agricultural workers with part-time temple duties. Members of the newly emerged group of specialist priests owed their welfare entirely to their temples that, mainly as the result of royal donations, were large landowners in their own right.

Before the beginning of the New Kingdom there was no standing army or police. The military only became a distinct social group during the New Kingdom. Some of them held other administrative or priestly positions, but many were entirely dependent on state resources. The two new groups, the priesthood and the military, were in direct competition for influence and resources with members of the traditional privileged section of society. This had a destabilising effect and was one of the major factors in the crisis that engulfed Egypt during the reign of Akhenaten.

Opposite: The god Amun-Ra crowning Queen Hatshepsut (1479–1457 BC). This is carved on the summit of a granite obelisk in the temple of Amun at Karnak.

Below: The southern part of the temple of Amun at Luxor, mainly built during the reign of Amenhotep III (1391–1353 BC).

ARTISTIC CONVENTIONS

Depictions of human figures and deities on the walls of Egyptian tombs and temples strike us as very unusual – this is due to their artistic conventions. The body is shown as a composite image, made up of different views of its parts (a similar approach was employed in modern art by Picasso). The face is almost always represented in profile, but the single eye is shown in front view. The shoulders are also seen from the front, but because the artist tried to show the important parts of the body unobscured, the left arm may be attached to the right shoulder and vice versa. From the shoulders down, the body turns into a three-quarter view of the waist, but the nipple is seen in profile. The legs are again in profile and the left foot is invariably shown in front of the right – the feet are always depicted resting on the same base line. Despite this "mosaic" way of viewing the human body, the overall impression is that of remarkably assured unity of composition.

EGYPTIAN RELIGION

Egyptian religion was polytheistic and multi-layered; the official religion of the temples was substantially different from the beliefs of ordinary people. It involved a very broad complex of ideas that also included explanations of the creation of the world and universe, the role of the pharaoh and his relation to society, and funerary beliefs concerning the afterlife. There was a multitude of deities that co-existed peacefully and could manifest themselves in a variety of forms. These could be anthropomorphic (a human form), such as the god Amun or the goddess Nut; partly or fully zoomorphic, for example, the god Anubis; or in other ways, for example the god Osiris is shown as a mummified human being. There were local gods, specific to particular areas, that represented the core of the Egyptian pantheon. Some of them acquired an importance that made them, in effect, state gods worshipped throughout the country, such as Amun of Thebes, the sun god Ra of Heliopolis (north-east of present-day Cairo) and Ptah of Memphis (south of Cairo). In the course of time, mythologies developed that tried to explain the relationships between some of these deities.

THE PHARAOH

The ideas that defined the king's position and role in society and religion appeared, like so many other things, in an almost complete form some time around 3000 BC. The characteristics of kingship remained remarkably stable throughout Egyptian history. Periods during which the king was unable to live up to expectations were times of profound ideological as well as political and economic crises. An important element of the religious revolution instigated by Tutankhamun's father, King Akhenaten, was a re-assessment of the role of the king and his family.

The word "pharaoh" derives from the Egyptian per-aa, "the great domain". This originally referred to royal properties, such as land, estates and workshops, and could be understood as "state property". It was during the reign of Akhenaten that per-aa was first used to refer to the king himself (in this book, the term pharaoh is used for kings of all periods).

Contrary to one of the most common popular misconceptions, the king was not a fully-fledged god. One of his many designations was netjer nefer, "the perfect god" or, possibly, "the junior god", in order to distinguish him from "senior gods", such as Amun, Ptah or Ra. In theory, his power was absolute, but in practice there were restraints imposed on him by both religion and tradition.

The king's right to rule over Egypt and the responsibilities that this entailed were conferred on him at his coronation. In Egyptian official religion, communication with the gods was his sole prerogative, although in practice many of his duties were carried out by priests. Administrative affairs at all levels were delegated to officials, first recruited from members of the royal family, but before long from commoners. His position as the ultimate mediator between the gods and the Egyptian people, however, was not enviable.

On the one hand, he was answerable to the gods for maintaining the maet, the Egyptian equivalent of law, order and tradition. It was his sacred duty to quell any internal unrest

Below: A larger than life-size, quartzite statue of Amenhotep III (1391–1353 BC), found in the temple of Amun at Luxor.

Opposite: A black granite statue of Thutmose IV (1401–1391 BC) and his mother Tia.

ROYAL TOMBS

The plan and external appearance of the royal tomb changed in response to developments in Egyptian religion and advances in technology. The earliest were rectangular structures built of sun-dried bricks, at first at Abydos in Upper Egypt, then at Saqqara. The first pyramid, that of King Djoser (2628–2609 BC) at Saqqara, was a stone-built, stepped structure. King Snofru (2573–2549 BC) built the first true pyramid at Dahshur. Practically all pyramids that served as royal tombs were situated in the area close to the ancient capital Memphis (south of modern Cairo), or a little further south, near El-Lisht. Between about 1550 and 1070 BC Egyptian kings were buried in the Valley of the Kings, on the west bank of the Nile opposite the city of Thebes (modern Luxor). These were rock-cut tombs with no obvious superstructures. The tombs of later kings were often made within the temple precincts in their home cities, such as Sais (modern Sa el-Hagar) in the case of the kings of the 26th dynasty.

as well as subdue any danger from abroad. On the other hand, he was responsible to his people for the smooth running of the world in the manner to which they were accustomed in their lifetime, and also how they expected it to run in death.

Some of this he was able to influence, such as maintaining the social order, efficient administration and the provision of offerings for tombs. The king also held responsibility for matters in which he was helpless, such as the regularity of cosmic events, the timely arrival of the Nile inundation and the size of the harvest. For these matters, he was expected to be able to ensure by his special relationship with the gods, which he safeguarded by maintaining their places of worship and the provision of offerings. A failure of the cosmos or nature was regarded as the failure of the pharaoh himself.

THE FIVE NAMES

The Egyptian king had five official names, which he received at his coronation. They were more than mere names, however, as they also expressed his relationship to the gods and some of the ambitions for his reign. The first three of these names may have been modified according to the purpose for which they were used; the last two were more stable.

The following are the names of Tutankhamun's grandfather, Amenhotep III:
1. The Horus name, which proclaimed the king as a visible form of the god Horus (sometimes written in a rectangular ornamental frame called serekh): Khaemmaet, "One who appeared as Truth".
2. The Two Ladies name, which conveyed his relationship with the vulture goddess Nekhbet and the cobra goddess Wadjet: Smenhepu-segerehtaui, "One who establishes the laws and pacifies the Two Lands".
3. The Golden Horus name, which probably described him as wearing the royal ceremonial dress and attributes: Aakhepesh-huysetjetiu, "One great of strength, the smiter of Asiatics".
4. The King of Upper and Lower Egypt name, which made him the ruler over Egypt: Nebmaetre, "The god Ra is the lord of Truth".
5. The Son of the God Ra name, which expressed his relationship to the sun god: Amenhotep-netjer-hekawaset, "The god Amun is satisfied, the god, the ruler of Thebes".

1. Khaemmaet: "One who appeared as Truth".

4. Nebmaetre, "The god Ra is the lord of Truth".

2. Smenhepu-segerehtaui: "One who establishes the laws and pacifies the Two Lands".

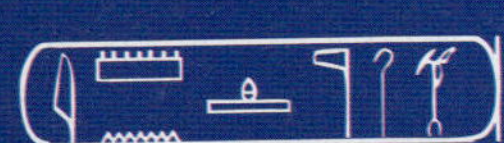

5. Amenhotep-netjer-hekawaset, "The god Amun is satisfied, the god, the ruler of Thebes".

3. Aakhepesh-huysetjetiu: "One great of strength, the smiter of Asiatics".

Below: A glazed steatite statuette of Queen Teye, the wife of Amenhotep III (1391–1353 BC). She was originally shown with her husband, but the figure of the king is almost completely lost.

Opposite: A traditional representation of an Egyptian pharaoh, Thutmose III (1479–1425 BC) massacring his enemies, carved in the temple of Amun in Karnak.

Akhenaten is famously notedfor abandoning traditional Egyptian polytheism and introducing worship on the Aten

KING AKHENATEN AND THE AMARNA PERIOD

The reign of King Amenhotep III, Tutankhamun's grandfather, which began in 1391 BC, led to unprecedented achievements in all spheres of Egyptian life. Externally, the country was secure, the economy was thriving and architecture and art flourished. It would have been difficult, therefore, to foresee the upheaval that was soon to engulf the country, but with hindsight it is possible to discern the signs of things to come.

Above: A polychrome glass vase in the form of a fish, from El-Amarna. Glass-making made rapid progress during the Amarna period.

Opposite: A Colossal statues addorsed against pillars in the early temples of the Aten at Karnak show Akhenaten's unusual physiognomy at its most extreme.

Society became unbalanced by the rapid growth of two particular social groups, which grew very influential – the priesthood and the military. There was also pressure for changes in the redistribution of available resources, but this was difficult to achieve without adjustments to the existing ideology (religion). Furthermore, Egypt was now a superpower that could no longer remain safely isolated from the rest of the ancient Near East. For this reason, the cult of the sun god, the deity best suited for universal worship, was gaining strength.

The situation came to a head with the accession of Amenhotep III's son of the same name, in 1353 BC. Amenhotep IV's physical appearance, perhaps due to a medical condition, was unusual and far from the masculine ideal of the Egyptian pharaoh. Straightaway, the new ruler began to show his preference for the sun god. The form that he chose was the Aten, represented impersonally by a sun disc with rays ending in human hands.

The King quickly became more radical, perhaps in response to the opposition to his reforms. He changed his name from Amenhotep ("The God Amun is Satisfied") to Akhenaten ("One Beneficial to the Aten"). He moved his residence and administrative capital to Middle Egypt, where he founded a new city and called it Akhetaten, "The Horizon of the Aten". The city is now El-Amarna, hence the term "Amarna period". New temples exclusively for the Aten were built there and in other parts of the country, while the cults of the other deities suffered neglect and, possibly, active persecution. It was, in effect, an attempt to introduce monotheism (the worship of one god) and this turned the traditional religious beliefs upside down. The consequences of Akhenaten's religious revolution were felt severely in the economic life of the country and in all sections of society.

Because Egyptian art served as an expression of religious ideas, it was profoundly affected. Iconography took its cue from Akhenaten's appearance, and portraiture was adjusted accordingly. The spoken language (called Late Egyptian by Egyptologists) began to be used in written communications.

The King's great supporter in his religious revolution was the chief queen, Nefertiti. They had six daughters (the third-eldest was Ankhesenpaten; she later changed her name to Ankhesenamun and became the queen of Tutankhamun), but, apparently, no sons.

The opposition to the changes must have been enormous, especially among the priesthood. The "Amarna revolution" petered out with the death of its two main protagonists, first Nefertiti, then Akhenaten in 1337 BC, and Akhenaten's successors were not strong enough to maintain the reforms.

THE TALATAT

Akhenaten's new deity, the Aten, was a special form of the sun god and the temples that were built for its worship were different from the traditional Egyptian sanctuaries. The main feature of their plan was a series of courts open to the sky. The traditional themes of temple decoration, especially those showing the king making offerings to various gods, were abandoned. The new Amarna repertory concentrated on the worship of the Aten and religious festivals, the King and his family and various activities connected with the royal residence. Akhenaten's builders employed smaller building blocks called talatat (from Arabic talata, "three", ie three handspans long) by Egyptologists.

The first was Smenkhkare, perhaps his son by a minor wife (like many other pharaohs, Akhenaten had several wives). When Smenkhkare's short reign came to an end, Tutankhaten ascended the throne at the tender age of about nine in 1336 BC. Before long, he was to become King Tutankhamun and to preside over the dismantling of Akhenaten's religious reforms.

Opposite, above: This relief shows King Akhenaten (left) kissing his eldest daughter Merytaten, while Queen Nefertiti has Meketaten seated on her lap and Ankhesenpaten (the future wife of Tutankhamun) on her shoulder.

Opposite, below: A limestone talatat with boats and stonemasons, decorated in sunk (carved below the surface of the stone) relief.

Right: A painted limestone bust of Queen Nefertiti, from a sculptor's studio at El-Amarna where it was probably used as a model for other sculptures of the Queen. Interestingly, it is curiously unaffected by the extreme artistic conventions of the Amarna period.

THE TOMB OF KING AKHENATEN

Akhenaten had a tomb made for himself and his family in a valley near his new royal residence at Akhetaten (El-Amarna). The tomb is rock-cut and differs from the earlier royal tombs in its plan (its main axis is straight and does not veer to the left) and in its decoration (there are, for example, mourning scenes and other unusual topics in the family part of the tomb). It seems that at least some members of the family, and possibly Akhenaten himself, were buried there. When Tutankhamun abandoned El-Amarna, the burials may have been transferred to the Valley of the Kings. Tomb KV 55 (KV stands for Kings' Valley), in the close vicinity of Tutankhamun's tomb, belonged to a member of the Amarna royal family, possibly Tutankhamun's predecessor Smenkhkare or even Akhenaten himself.

THE DECIPHERMENT OF THE HIEROGLYPHS

The hieroglyphic script appeared around 3000 BC and was used until the end of the 4th century ad (the last inscription dates from ad 394). Thereafter, it was not just the ability to read and write hieroglyphs that was lost completely, but also the principles of the script. Because hieroglyphs are recognisable pictures it was thought that the writing was pictorial and allegorical and recorded concepts rather than letters, words and sentences. Hieroglyphica, a treatise written by Horapollo (an Egyptian writer and philosopher in the late 5th century), proved to be a major contributor to this particular misunderstanding.

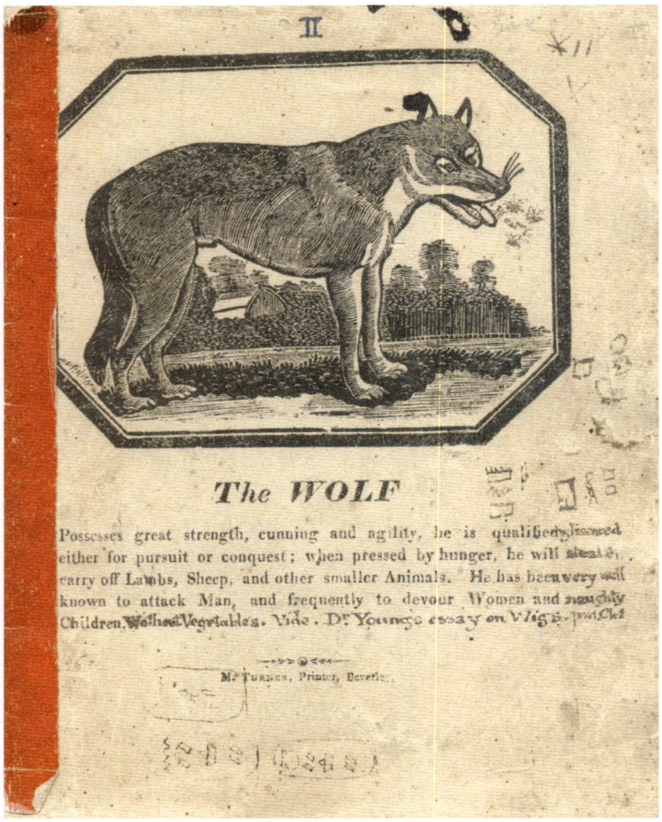

In the succeeding centuries, various Moslem scholars, such as Jabir Ibn Hayan (7th to 8th centuries), Ibn Wahshiyah (probably 9th or 10th centuries) and Abu Al-Qasim Al-Iraqi (13th to 14th centuries), made important, although not entirely successful, attempts at understanding Egyptian inscriptions. Unfortunately, their efforts remained unknown in Europe. Horapollo's mistaken interpretation of hieroglyphs was accepted and further elaborated on by other scholars, such as Athanasius Kircher (1602–80) in the 17th century. An early list of Egyptian hieroglyphs, mainly based on monuments brought to England during the 17th and 18th centuries, was published by Alexander Gordon in 1737–9.

A new and decisive impetus to the solution of the riddle was provided by the discovery of an inscription written in two languages (Egyptian and Greek) and three scripts (hieroglyphic, a cursive form of writing called demotic used from the mid-

Opposite: Hieroglyphs of the Old Kingdom. The text of a will endowing a tomb near the pyramid of Khephren at Giza, dating from mid-Dynasty V (c.2400 BC).

Left and below: Sir William Gell (1777–1830) copied hieroglyphs on Egyptian monuments situated in Italy into his notebooks and corresponded with Young and Champollion in an attempt to discover how to read them.

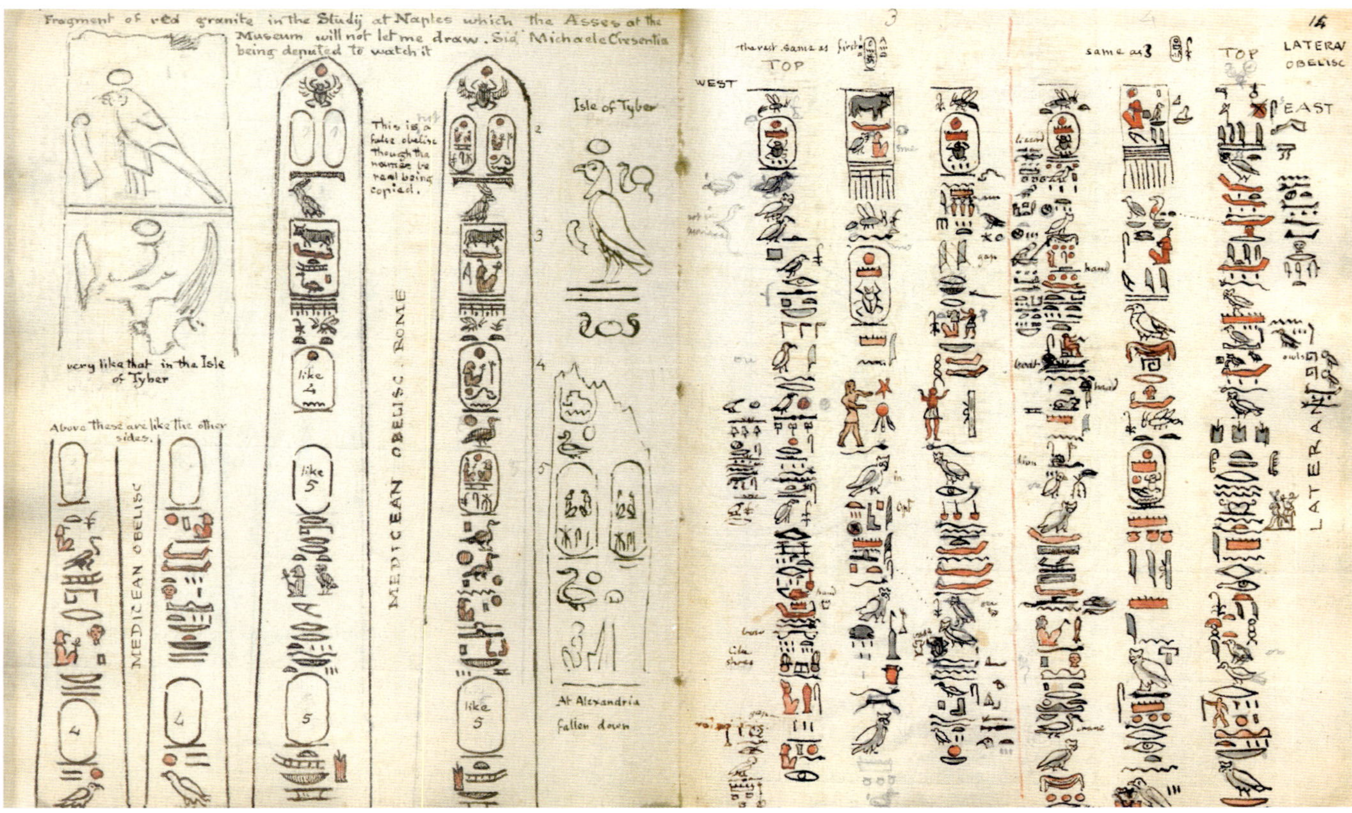

THE HIERATIC SCRIPT

The relationship between hieroglyphs and the hieratic script is similar to that between modern-day printed text and handwriting. Scribes used a reed pen and ink for writing on papyri and the same method was employed for brief texts on jars to indicate their contents and the date and name of the person responsible.

Above: These hieroglyphs of the Ramessid period are a religious text from the tomb of Ramesses VI (1143–1136 BC) in the Valley of the Kings.

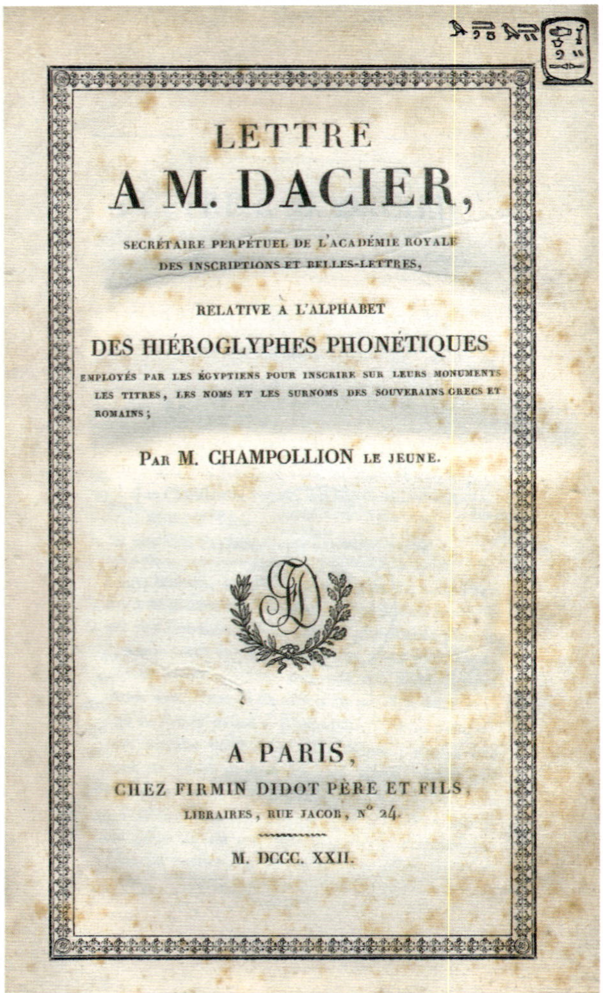

LETTRE
A M. DACIER,
SECRÉTAIRE PERPÉTUEL DE L'ACADÉMIE ROYALE
DES INSCRIPTIONS ET BELLES-LETTRES,
RELATIVE A L'ALPHABET
DES HIÉROGLYPHES PHONÉTIQUES
EMPLOYÉS PAR LES ÉGYPTIENS POUR INSCRIRE SUR LEURS MONUMENTS LES TITRES, LES NOMS ET LES SURNOMS DES SOUVERAINS GRECS ET ROMAINS;
PAR M. CHAMPOLLION LE JEUNE.
A PARIS,
CHEZ FIRMIN DIDOT PÈRE ET FILS,
LIBRAIRES, RUE JACOB, Nº 24.
M. DCCC. XXII.

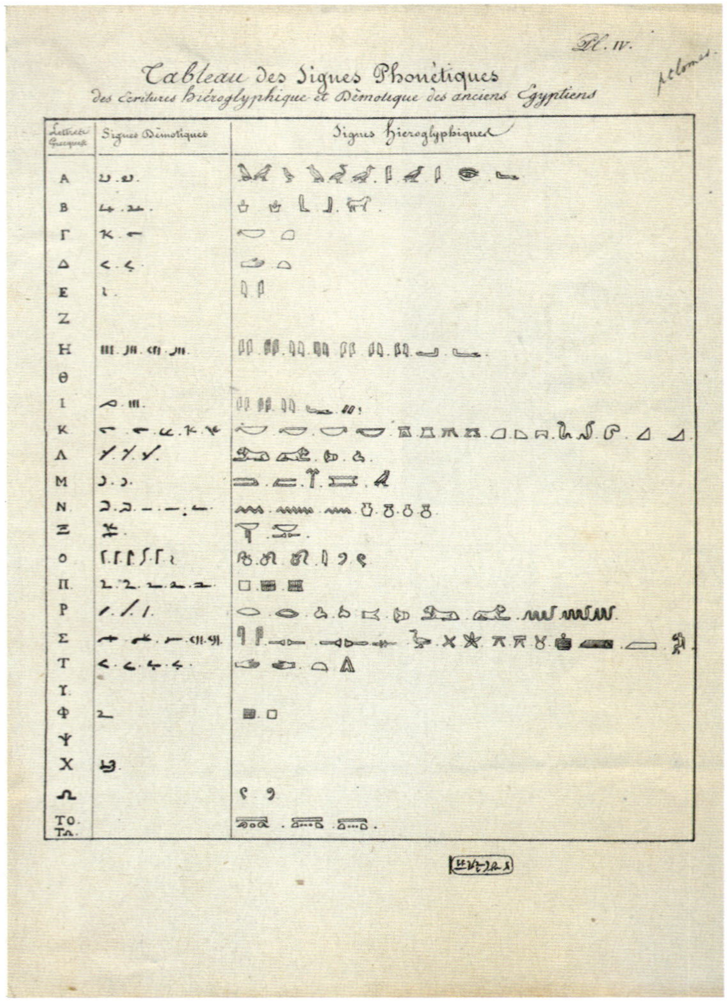

17th century BC, and Greek) at El-Rashid (Rosetta) in the north-western Nile Delta. This was in 1799, during Napoleon's ill-fated invasion of Egypt. The monument, now known as the Rosetta Stone, is a decree of year nine of Ptolemy V Epiphanes (196 BC) and of little historical importance in itself.

It was the demotic section of the Rosetta Stone that at first received most attention from scholars, such as the Frenchman Silvestre de Sacy and especially the Swede J D Åkerblad. An important advance was made when it was recognised that the hieroglyphic and demotic parts of the text were closely related and that they both contained phonetic elements (signs denoting sounds). A major contribution to this was made by the brilliantly versatile English scholar Thomas Young (1773–1829). He also confirmed a suggestion, which had already been made by earlier researchers, that the oval frames (cartouches) in the hieroglyphic script contain the names of Ptolemaic kings and queens. Young was able to read several of them, but, although on the right track, he did not pursue his ideas to their logical conclusion.

Above: An extract from Champollion's Lettre à M Dacier, published in 1822 and represents the beginning of the correct understanding of Egyptian hieroglyphs. The hieroglyphic inscription on the title page (left) was made by Champollion for a friend and says "to my friend Dubois".

Left: Jean-François Champollion (1790–1832), the French scholar who deciphered Egyptian hieroglyphs.

THE HIEROGLYPHS

Three types of writing were used throughout pharaonic history for recording the Egyptian language: hieroglyphic script, hieratic and demotic. Hieroglyphs (from the Greek hieros, "sacred", and gluphe, "carving") were used for monumental purposes and carved or incised on objects (rather than written in ink with a pen). They are representations of people, animals and birds, trees and plants, celestial bodies and various other objects, but they are not picture writing. Although there are some hieroglyphs where the picture is identical to its "meaning", many others have a sound value or perform a particular function in the writing system. As a rule, only consonants were recorded. Some of the hieroglyphs may represent one consonant, others a combination of two or more. Hieroglyphs could be written in horizontal lines from right to left (the main direction of writing), from left to right or in vertical columns facing right or left. Divisions between words and sentences were not indicated.

The fame of the decipherment of the hieroglyphic script therefore went to Jean-François Champollion (1790–1832), a French scholar. His attempts at decipherment of hieroglyphs were helped considerably by his knowledge of Coptic, the last stage of Egyptian written in Greek characters. He demonstrated that not only the hieroglyphic signs in the cartouches on the Rosetta Stone, but also other hieroglyphic inscriptions must be read phonetically (alphabetically). Champollion correctly read the name of Ramesses II, copied at Abu Simbel and the cartouche of King Thutmose. His discovery was made public in his Lettre à M Dacier relative à l'alphabet des hiéroglyphes phonétiques, which was read at the French Academy on 29 September 1822. Much remained to be done before Egyptian inscriptions could be read with some confidence, but we can regard this day as the birthday of scholarly Egyptology.

Above, left: Thomas Young (1773–1829), the scholar who nearly succeeded in deciphering the hieroglyphs.

Above, right: Hieroglyphs from the end of the 18th Dynasty on a stela of King Haremhab (1323–1295 BC), from his tomb at Saqqara.

Middle: These hieroglyphs of the early Ptolemaic period appear inlaid in glass on the wooden coffin of the priest Pedusiri. From Tuna el-Gebel, c.320 BC.

Right: The Rosetta Stone, a decree of year nine of Ptolemy V Epiphanes (196 BC), is inscribed in hieroglyphs, demotic and Greek.

REDISCOVERING MONUMENTS OF ANCIENT EGYPT

Political, as well as scholarly, factors affected the development of Egyptology in the first half of the 19th century. Napoleon's expedition at the end of the 18th century brought Egypt to the attention of the Western world and Muhammad Ali, the new viceroy of Egypt, opened the country to European entrepreneurs as well as scholars and tourists.

Opposite: The statue of a scribe dating from about 2450 BC, found by Auguste Mariette during his excavations at Saqqara.

Above: The quartzite head of a colossal statue of Amenhotep III (1391–1353 BC), which was removed from the King's cult temple at Thebes on the instructions of Henry Salt.

Archaeological exploration of Egypt during the 19th century can be divided into three periods. The main characteristic of the first, before 1850, was a largely unregulated search for antiquities in order to satisfy the demands of European collectors and museums. Crude digging for antiquities, rather than excavations, with little or no recording was carried out by dealers. Diplomats resident in Egypt were in an ideal position to become involved in such excavations for antiquarian as well as financial reasons, and national museums of major European countries were only too keen to take the objects off their hands.

The "Padua strong man" Giovanni Battista Belzoni (1778–1823) excavated at Giza, Thebes (Karnak, the Ramesseum and the Valley of the Kings) and Abu Simbel, mostly for the British Consul-General Henry Salt (1780–1827). Salt, who was genuinely interested in ancient Egypt, also employed another colourful Italian, Giovanni Battista Caviglia (1770–1845) to work at Giza and Mit Rahina. Many of the monuments assembled by Salt now form a very important part of the Egyptian collections in the British Museum in London and in the Louvre in Paris. Monuments acquired from Salt's rival, the French Consul-General Bernardino Drovetti (1776–1852), are in the

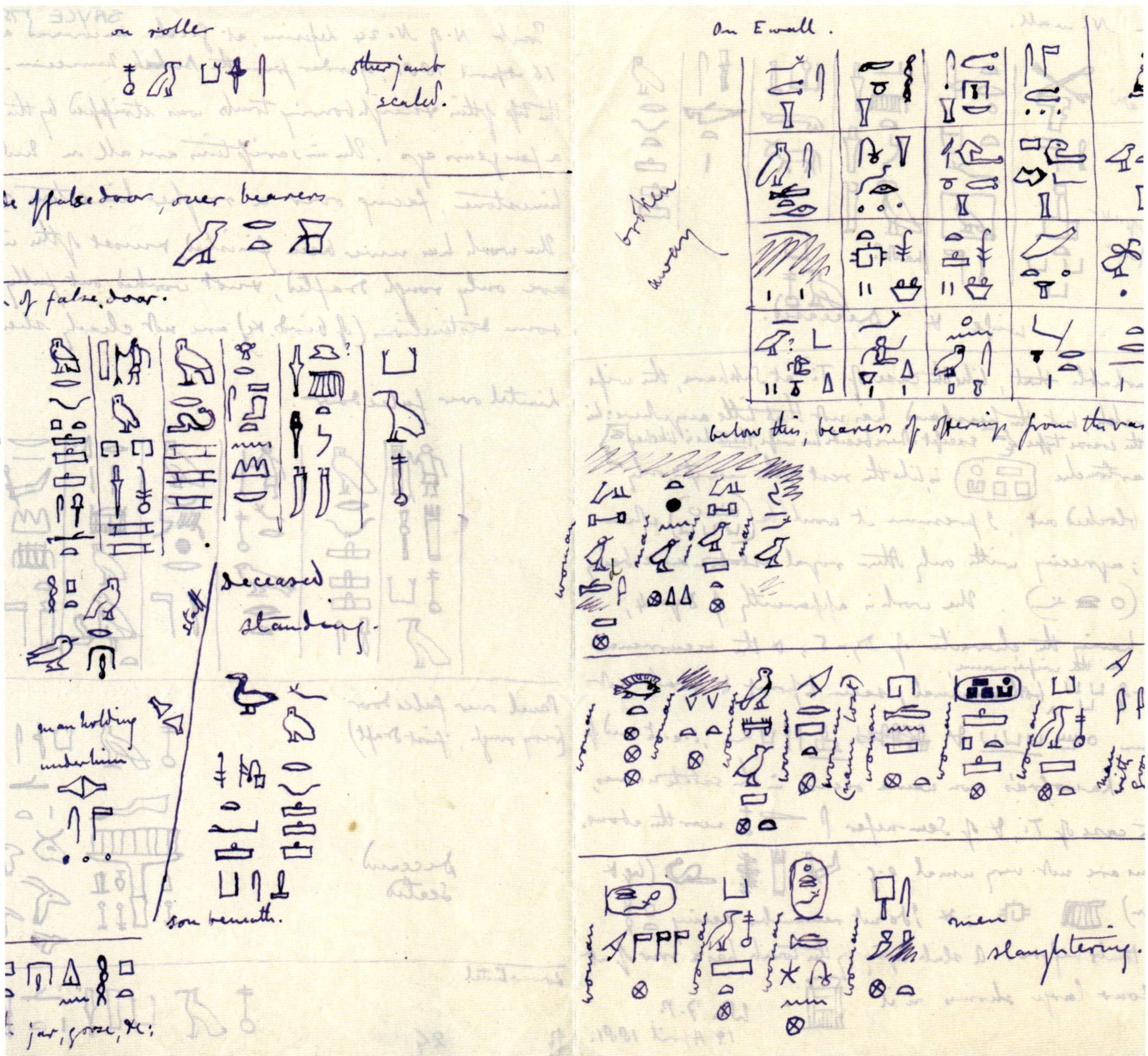

Louvre, the Museo Egizio in Turin and the Ägyptisches Museum in Berlin.

The second period, between about 1850 and 1880, saw the beginnings of organised archaeology. It was dominated by the French archaeologist Auguste Mariette, the excavator of the Serapeum at Saqqara. Mariette excavated on a large scale and at a number of important archaeological sites simultaneously. He was appointed Director of Egyptian Monuments by Khedive Said in 1858 and under his guidance the first Museum of Egyptian Antiquities at Bulaq in Cairo was created in 1863. Methodologically, the little known excavations directed by Joseph Hekekyan (1807–75) at Heliopolis and Mit Rahina in the early 1850s were also very important.

The era of modern archaeological excavations and archaeological recording began in about 1880. the most remarkable excavator of this period was Sir William Matthew Flinders Petrie (1853–1942). He came to Egypt in 1880 with a main interest in metrology and the measurements of the pyramids, but he soon became the foremost archaeologist

Opposite: Notes by A C Harris (1790–1869) in which he identified the Memphite Serapeum several years before Auguste Mariette.

Right: The Ptolemaic section of the Serapeum at Saqqara, discovered by Auguste Mariette.

Below: A granite statue of the Vizier Paser kneeling with a figure of the god Ptah, c.1275 BC. It was found by J Hekekyan at Mit Rahina.

MARIETTE AND THE SERAPEUM

In the summer of 1850, a young French Egyptologist, Auguste Mariette (1821–81), came to Egypt on a mission to acquire Coptic, Ethiopic and Syriac manuscripts. In the gardens of Alexandrian and Cairene houses, Mariette saw a number of sphinxes, which had apparently been dug up at Saqqara by a Cairo dealer called Fernandez. On his visit to Saqqara, Mariette came across a sphinx partly showing above the sand. Hieroglyphs on a stone nearby contained the name of Osiris-Apis. In a flash of inspiration he was reminded of a passage in Strabo's Geography about the approach to the Memphite temple of the god Serapis, and concluded that his discovery must have been this monument (the same suggestion had been made by A C Harris in 1848, but there is no reason to doubt that both scholars reached their conclusions independently). Mariette began to excavate using the money intended for the purchase of manuscripts and eventually confirmed the theory in spectacular fashion by discovering the Serapeum – the burial place of the sacred Apis-bulls, linked to the chief Memphite god Ptah.

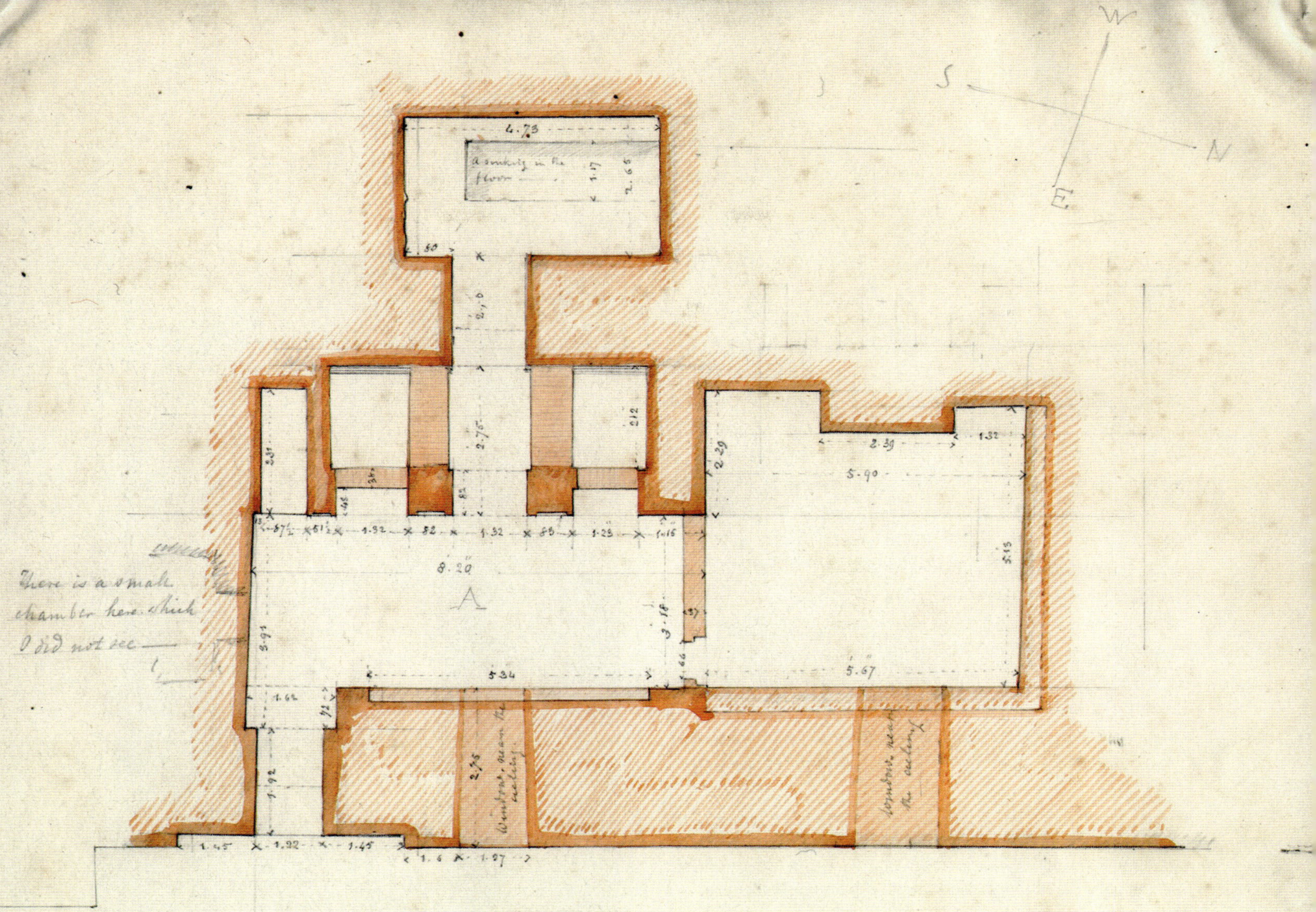

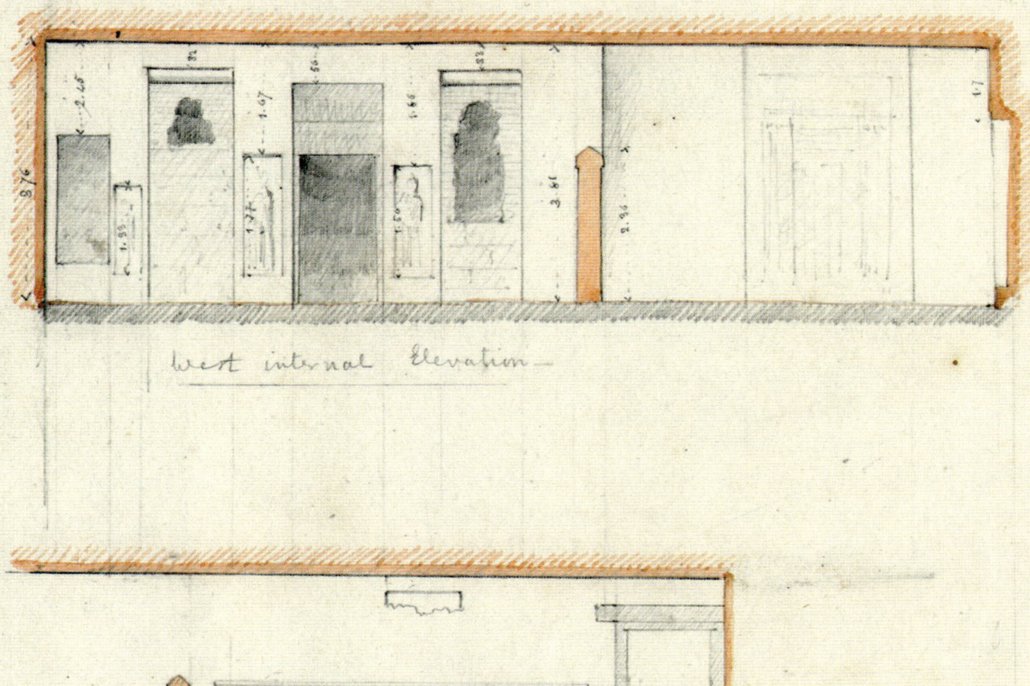

West internal Elevation

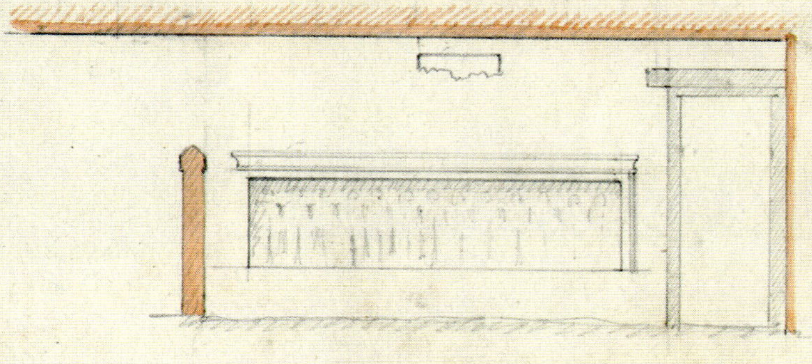

Elevation of the East Side of the Room A, with the niche which contained 13 broken figures

JOSEPH HEKEKYAN

Joseph Hekekyan (1807–75) was an Armenian civil engineer who excavated at Mit Rahina (Memphis), on the west bank of the Nile south of Cairo, in 1852 and 1854. The work was financed by the Egyptian Government at the suggestion of Leonard Horner of the Geological Society. Its aim was geological, rather than archaeological: to investigate the rate of formation of alluvial land in the Nile Valley by excavating around monuments of a known date. However, the excavation turned out to be of profound importance for the history of Ramessid Memphis. This work was probably the first properly recorded stratified excavation in Egypt.

working in Egypt. Some of the methods that he employed were far ahead of most of his contemporaries.

In 1881, a cache containing mummies of some of the most famous pharaohs was discovered accidentally by local inhabitants at Deir el-Bahri and published by Gaston Maspero (1846–1916), the Director of the Antiquities Service. In 1891, under Maspero's successor, Eugène Grébaut (1846–1915), the communal burial of the priests of Amun was found at Bab el-Gasus at Deir el-Bahri. In the same year, the young Howard Carter arrived in Egypt.

Opposite: J W Wild's (1814–92) record of excavations made at Giza by the expedition led by K R Lepsius in 1842–5.

Left: King Sety I (1294–1279 BC) before the goddess Hathor, in his tomb in the Valley of the Kings. Discovered by G B Belzoni, this contemporary copy was made by A Ricci.

Above: The colossal statue of Ramesses II (1279–1213 BC). Discovered in the temple of the god Ptah at Mit Rahina by G B Caviglia.

RECORDING MONUMENTS OF ANCIENT EGYPT

At first, Jean-François Champollion's decipherment of the hieroglyphic script in 1822 was not received favourably by everybody. Even when it gained acceptance, it was clear that it was necessary to collect material on which the newly acquired knowledge could be tested and from which further information on Ancient Egypt could be gathered. The existing copies of inscriptions, including the Napoleonic Description de l'Egypte, were not sufficient.

Above: G A Hoskins' copy of agricultural scenes in the tomb of Paheri, from c.1470 BC, at El-Kab.

Opposite: E W Lane's drawing of the entrance to the Great Pyramid of Khufu (2549-2526 BC) at Giza, achieved with the help of a camera lucida.

The development of Egyptian epigraphy (copying inscriptions and scenes in tombs and temples) parallels, to some extent, the progress of excavations. It became Egyptology's main focus of scholarly attention during the first half of the 19th century. This was the pioneering era. Henry Salt (1780–1827), the British Consul-General in Egypt, became famous as an avid collector of antiquities, but he was also a keen copyist. He was one of the first to overcome the restrictions imposed on him by his training in the Western artistic tradition and so produce almost completely faithful copies of ancient Egyptian monuments.

Sir John Gardner Wilkinson (1797–1875), who came to Egypt in 1821, was a compulsive copyist for whom nothing was too insignificant to record. He left a huge amount of material, still unpublished, and in this he was rivalled by Robert Hay (1799–1863), James Burton (1788–1862) and W J Bankes (1786–1855). Their copies also still await publication.

Jean-François Champollion (1790–1832) organised his own epigraphic expedition to Egypt in 1828–9 and in this he was

AMELIA EDWARDS

Amelia Edwards (1831–92) made her first trip to Egypt and Syria in 1873–4. During her visit she produced a number of accomplished watercolours. Although they were not intended to be accurate records, they are interesting because some of them show monuments before extensive, but little recorded, restorations. The plight of Egyptian monuments led Amelia Edwards to become the founder of the Egypt Exploration Fund (now Egypt Exploration Society) in 1882.

Above: This watercolour by Amelia Edwards shows the temple at Dakka, dating from the Ptolemaic and Roman periods, in Nubia.

Below: E Hawker's watercolour showing the obelisk at Alexandria, which is now re-erected in Central Park in New York.

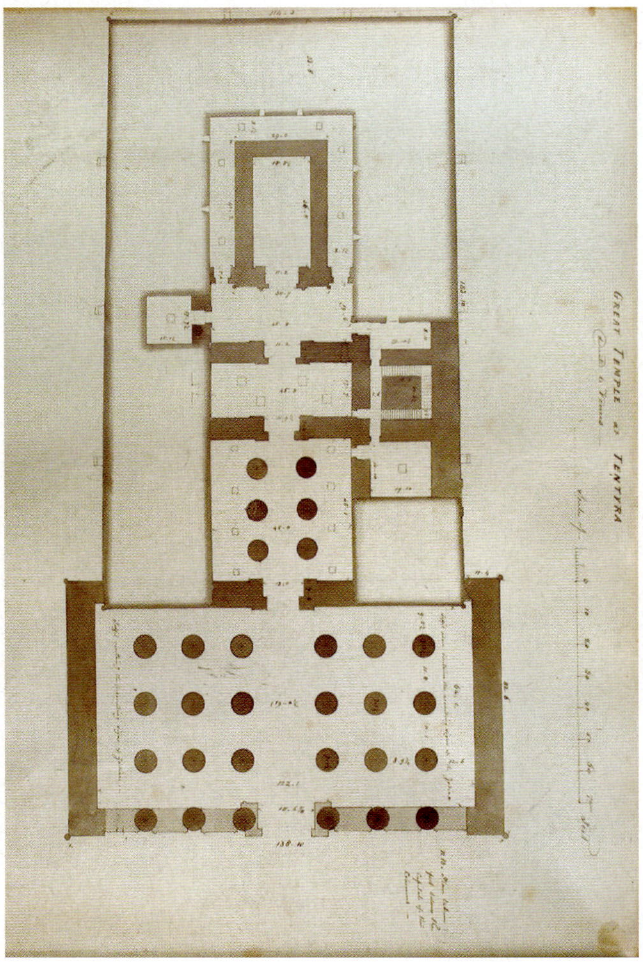

Top and above: E W Lane, best known for his Arabic dictionary, recorded the Giza Sphinx and the obelisk at Alexandria with the help of a camera lucida.

Left: Charles Barry (1795–1860) was one of the first to make accurate plans of Egyptian monuments (here the temple of Hathor at Dendera) in 1818–9.

assisted by the Italian Egyptologist Ippolito Rosellini (1800-43). Other important French epigraphists were Nestor L'Hôte (1804-42) and Prisse d'Avennes (1807-79). The great German Egyptologist Richard Lepsius (1810-84) was the head of a large Prussian Expedition to Egypt and Nubia in 1842-5 and this set the standards for Egyptian epigraphy, which remained valid until about 1890.

But there were many others, less well-known, who may not have been Egyptologists and could not read hieroglyphs, but who, nevertheless, left extremely valuable copies, drawings and watercolours showing Egyptian sites and monuments before they suffered depredation due to ill-treatment, tourism and modern development. Among them were Edward W. Lane (1801-76), better known for his contribution to Islamic studies, the artists G A Hoskins (1802-63) and Edward Hawker (fl. 1850-2), and the architect Hector Horeau (1801-72). Because so many Egyptian monuments have been damaged or destroyed in the past two centuries, any 19th-century record is worth preserving because it may provide information that is not available anywhere else.

The next period saw a further increase in epigraphic activities, which now took advantage of the large-scale clearances of major temples in Upper Egypt. Auguste Mariette, Heinrich Brugsch (1827-94) and Emmanuel de Rougé (1811-72) were particularly active in this field.

In 1881, Heinrich and Emile Brugsch (1842-1930) discovered the Pyramid Texts, a huge corpus of texts inscribed inside some late Old Kingdom pyramids. Only a little later, the Frenchman Albert Gayet (1856-1916) at Luxor, and Howard Carter (1874-1939) at Deir el-Bahri, further refined the standards of Egyptian epigraphy and brought them close to those that are practised today.

HECTOR HOREAU

Hector Horeau (1801-72) was a French architect who travelled through Egypt and Lower Nubia in 1839 and produced many remarkably detailed plans, sections and watercolours. These contain many features that attracted him as an architect, but that other painters or watercolourists would have ignored. Most of them were published as Panorama d'Egypte et de Nubie in 1842.

Above, right: Sailing boats, viticultural scenes, a scribe handing in a list and men bringing chests with linen, in the tomb of Fetekti, from c.2350 BC, at Saqqara. These copies were made by the expedition led by R Lepsius.

Above, left: The temples at Abu Simbel, from the reign of Ramesses II (1279-1213 BC), in watercolour by Hector Horeau.

CARTER AND CARNARVON

Howard Carter was born at 10 Rich Terrace in Kensington, London on 9 May 1874, but his childhood was spent in his parents' hometown – Swaffham in Norfolk. It was there that he also received a very modest private education. His father, Samuel John Carter, was a fairly successful artist, known for his animal paintings, and Howard inherited his talent.

Opposite: Howard Carter's watercolour sketches of birds (vulture, hawk and pintail duck) in hieroglyphs and in real life.

Above: The 5th Earl of Carnarvon (1866–1923), an aristocrat with a passion for Egyptian archaeology.

As is often the case, Carter was brought to Egyptian archaeology more by accident than by deliberate planning. Didlington Hall near Swaffham was the seat of the Amhersts and boasted one of the largest private collections of Egyptian antiquities in England (this was eventually sold at Sotheby's in 1922). One of Lord Amherst's friends was the Egyptologist P E Newberry who, in 1890, began recording tombs in Middle Egypt on behalf of the London-based Egypt Exploration Fund (now the Egypt Exploration Society). In the autumn of 1891, when he was still only 17, Carter was hired to work as a "tracer" (copyist) with Newberry at Beni Hasan and Deir el-Bersha. A few months later, he joined Flinders Petrie at El-Amarna and got a first taste of real Egyptian archaeology. This was the beginning of a decade of work on the Fund's projects. From 1893 until 1899 he was responsible for recording the inscriptions and scenes in the temple of Queen Hatshepsut at Deir el Bahri.

During the next stage of his professional career, Carter, now a recognised archaeologist, worked for the Egyptian Antiquities Service. In 1900, he was appointed Chief Inspector of Antiquities with responsibilities for Upper Egypt, which included Luxor and the Valley of the Kings. Ther

TELL EL-BALAMUN

In 1913, Howard Carter and Lord Carnarvon conducted a season of excavations at Tell el-Balamun in the northern Delta, some 19km (nearly 12 miles) from the Mediterranean shore, close to the Damietta branch of the Nile. They identified a palace and temple enclosure and the remains of a town of the Greco-Roman period (after 332 BC). Small finds included pottery, scarabs, faience amulets, granite weights, a fragment of a stela inscribed in demotic, a small statuette, jewellery and Roman glass and coins, but this was not sufficiently rewarding for the excavators and work was discontinued.

corresponding post supervising the Delta and Lower Egypt.

Who knows what heights in the Antiquities Service Carter could have attained had it not been for an incident at Saqqara that produced a physical confrontation between a party of arrogant European visitors and the Service's Egyptian employees? Carter was not personally involved, but his unflinching support for his men in the face of massive pressure from all sides brought, in effect, his career in the Service to an end. His action is regarded as highly principled by some and foolhardy by others. He left the Antiquities Service the following year, in 1905.

The next four years were dispiriting and little more than marking time. He was odd-jobbing as a draftsman for other archaeologists, painted some watercolours and used his Egyptological knowledge to help with acquisitions of antiquities.

But fortune favours the brave and obstinate. In 1905, the Earl of Carnarvon visited Egypt in search of a climate that would help his recovery following a serious car accident. He became very interested in Egyptian archaeology and decided to finance some excavations. The Antiquities Service, however, insisted that he should work with an experienced archaeologist. Carter was the best person available.

The year 1909 marked the first cooperation between a brilliantly intuitive archaeologist and an English aristocrat with a passion for archaeology. The wheel of fortune was

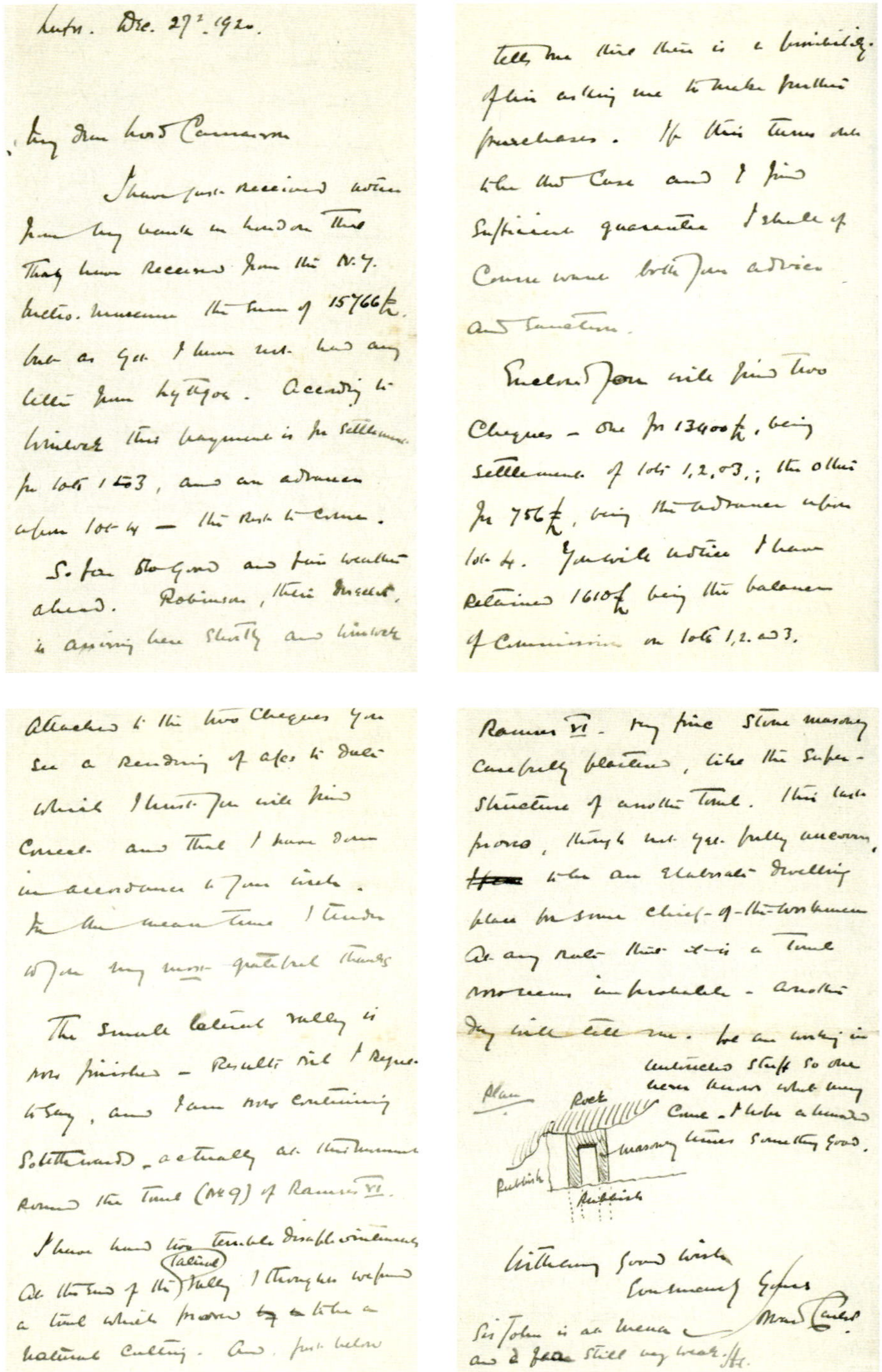

Luxor. Dec. 27th. 1920.

My dear Lord Carnarvon

I have just received notice from my bank in London that they have received from the N.Y. Metro. Museum the sum of 15766£. but as yet I have not had any letter from Lythgoe. According to his note this payment is for settlement for lots 1 to 3, and an advance upon lot 4 — the rest to come.

So far so good and fair weather ahead. Robinson, their Director, is arriving here shortly and his note tells me that there is a possibility of his asking me to make further purchases. If this turns out to be the case and I find sufficient guarantee I shall of course want both your advice and sanction.

Enclosed you will find two Cheques – one for 13400£. being settlement of lots 1,2, & 3.; the other for 756£. being the advance upon lot 4. You will notice I have retained 1610£ being the balance of Commission on lots 1,2. & 3.

Attached to the two Cheques you see a rendering of a/cs to date which I trust you will find correct and that I have done in accordance to your wish. In the mean time I tender to you my most grateful thanks.

The small lateral valley is now finished – Results nil I regret to say, and I am now continuing southward – actually at this moment round the Tomb (No 9) of Rameses VI. I have had two terrible disappointments. At the end of the (lateral) valley I thought we found a tomb which proved to be a natural cutting. And just below Rameses VI. very fine stone masonry carefully plastered, like the super-structure of another tomb. This latter proves, though not yet fully uncovered, to be an elaborate dwelling place for some chief-of-the-workmen. At any rate that it is a tomb now seems improbable – another day will tell me. We are working in untouched stuff so one never knows what may come. I hope a hundred times something good.

Plan
Rock
masonry
Rubbish
Rubbish

With every good wish
Continually yours
Howard Carter.

Sir John is at Mena and I fear still very weak. HC.

Opposite, left: Excavations at Tell el-Balamun in 1913. Women and girls were employed as basket carriers, removing the excavated soil.

Opposite, right: Howard Carter (right) and Lord Carnarvon during the Tell el-Balamun excavations.

Right: A letter from Howard Carter to Lord Carnarvon, dated 27 December 1920, about excavations near the tomb of Ramesses VI (KV 9). The tomb of Tutankhamun was discovered close by two years later.

CARTER'S BIRDS AND ANIMALS

Howard Carter was a very keen observer of Egyptian animal and bird life - notes about encounters with animals can be found even in his excavation journals. He was also very interested in the way the Egyptians depicted them in scenes in tombs and temples and in hieroglyphs.

again beginning to turn Carter's way. The Carter-Carnarvon work began at Asasif in the Theban necropolis. In 1912, they moved to Sakha in the Delta and the following year to Tell el-Balamun. Both of them were keen to work in the Valley of the Kings, but permission to excavate there had been granted to the American archaeologist Theodore M Davis.

It was not until 1914, after Davis's retirement, that Lord Carnarvon was allowed to excavate in the Valley of the Kings. The scene was now set for one of the greatest archaeological discoveries and Carter's ultimate vindication. It is a curious fact that if it had not been for his stubborn support of his Egyptian staff after the fracas at Saqqara, he probably would not have become the discoverer of Tutankhamun.

Above, left: A watercolour showing a landscape at Thebes by Howard Carter. It used to hang on a wall in his house at Elwet el-Diban during hiswork on the tomb of Tutankhamun.

Above, right: One of Howard Carter's watercolours showing an ibex.

Opposite above: A hawk copied by Howard Carter at Deir el-Bahri in 1895.

Opposite, left: A scene showing an Egyptian expedition sent to the Land of Punt, somewhere on the Somali coast of Africa. It was copied by Howard Carter in the temple of Queen Hatshepsut (1479–1457 BC) at Deir el-Bahri in 1897.

Opposite, right: A portrait of Howard Carter, painted by his brother William in 1924.

BACK IN THE VALLEY

Howard Carter's wish to return to the Valley of the Kings came true on 8 February 1915. Ten years after his less than amicable departure from the Antiquities Service, the occasion must have been particularly satisfying. Later, he wrote that finding the tomb of Tutankhamun was his greatest desire, but the generally held opinion at that time was that the remains of funerary equipment found in 1909 were all that was left of Tutankhamun's burial.

Above: A photograph of Howard Carter's excavations taken on 17 January 1920.
Opposite: Workmen removing debris over the entrance to the tomb of Tutankhamun.

The valley stands on the on the west bank of the Nile within the heart of the Thebian Necropolis

Carter may not necessarily have shared this view, but there was little to indicate where the tomb might have been. He used his intimate knowledge of the Valley of the Kings to explore areas that had been neglected by earlier archaeologists and his brilliant intuition in the search for an undiscovered royal tomb. One can detect signs of his growing impatience and, eventually, frustration as successive seasons of work were not yielding the desired result. But, as always throughout his career, Carter's determination eventually won through.

The first short season of excavations, near the tomb of Amenhotep III (KV 22), produced moderately interesting results, but Carter was after a bigger quarry. When the next campaign began on 1 December 1917, he focused on a small lateral wadi between tombs KV 7 (Ramesses II) and KV 9 (Ramesses VI). His instinct was right; the tomb of Tutankhamun would be found close to the mouth of it, although in the main Valley, some five years later. Small objects that were discovered represented the spoils of a large building site as well as items removed from royal tombs and abandoned by tomb robbers. Ostraca (flakes of smooth limestone) inscribed with the hieratic script by ancient scribes documenting the work on royal tombs were especially numerous. Huts that originally housed workmen employed in the work on royal tombs were also a feature of the area.

Not satisfied with the results, Carter moved his workmen deeper into the Valley, to the tomb of Thutmose I (KV 38), for

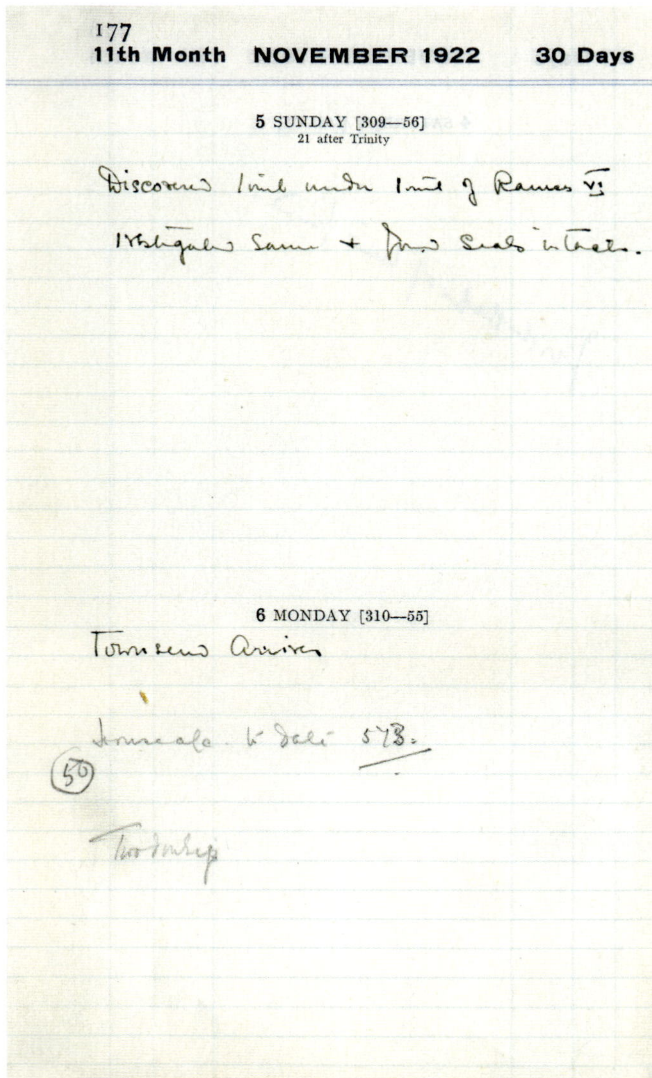
177
11th Month NOVEMBER 1922 30 Days

5 SUNDAY [309—56]
21 after Trinity

Discovered tomb under tomb of Ramses VI

6 MONDAY [310—55]

Above: The first signs of the steps that descend to the tomb entrance.

Right and opposite: Pages from Howard Carter's pocket diary for 1922, in which he recorded the discovery and opening of the tomb of Tutankhamun.

EMBALMING MATERIALS

Materials that came into contact with the body during mummification were not simply discarded, but were buried in the vicinity of the tomb. A cache (numbered as KV 54) containing bags of natron (dehydrating agent), pieces of linen bearing the name of Tutankhamun, pottery vessels, flower collars, seal impressions and a small mummy mask were found in the Valley of the Kings by Theodore M Davis in 1907–8. It seems, however, that this may have been a reburial following one of the robberies of Tutankhamun's tomb and not the place where the material was originally deposited.

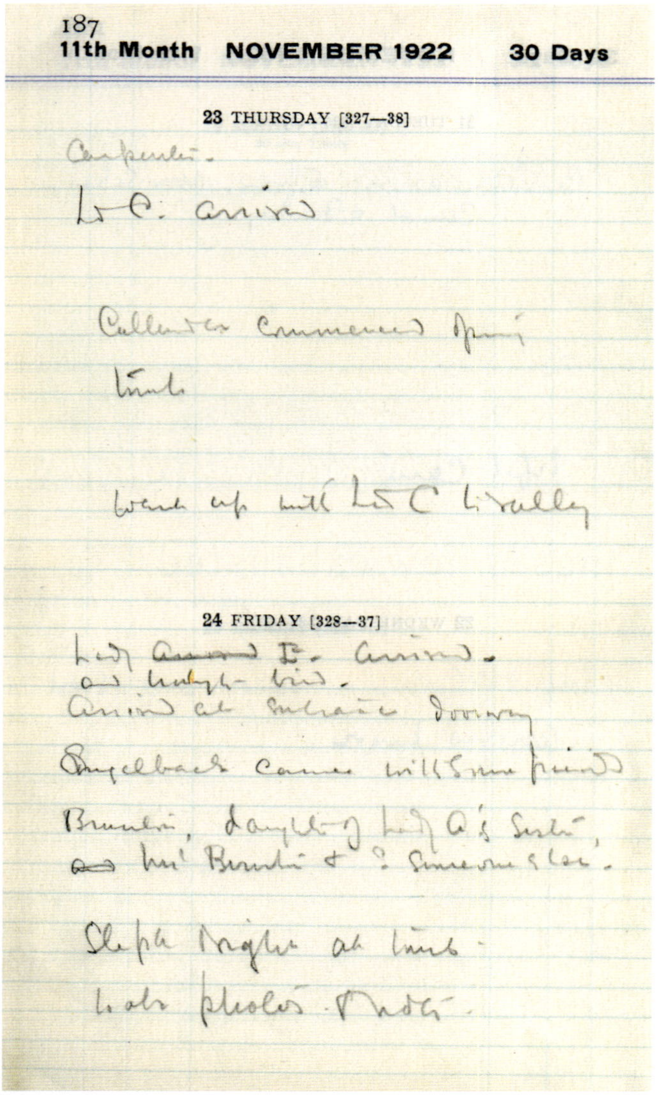

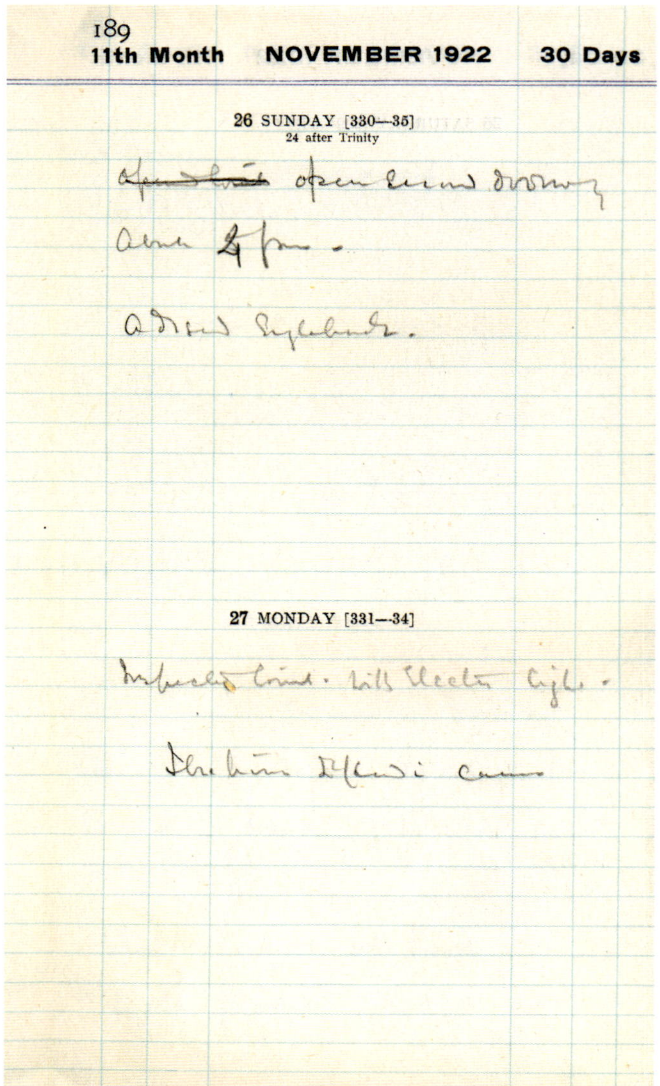

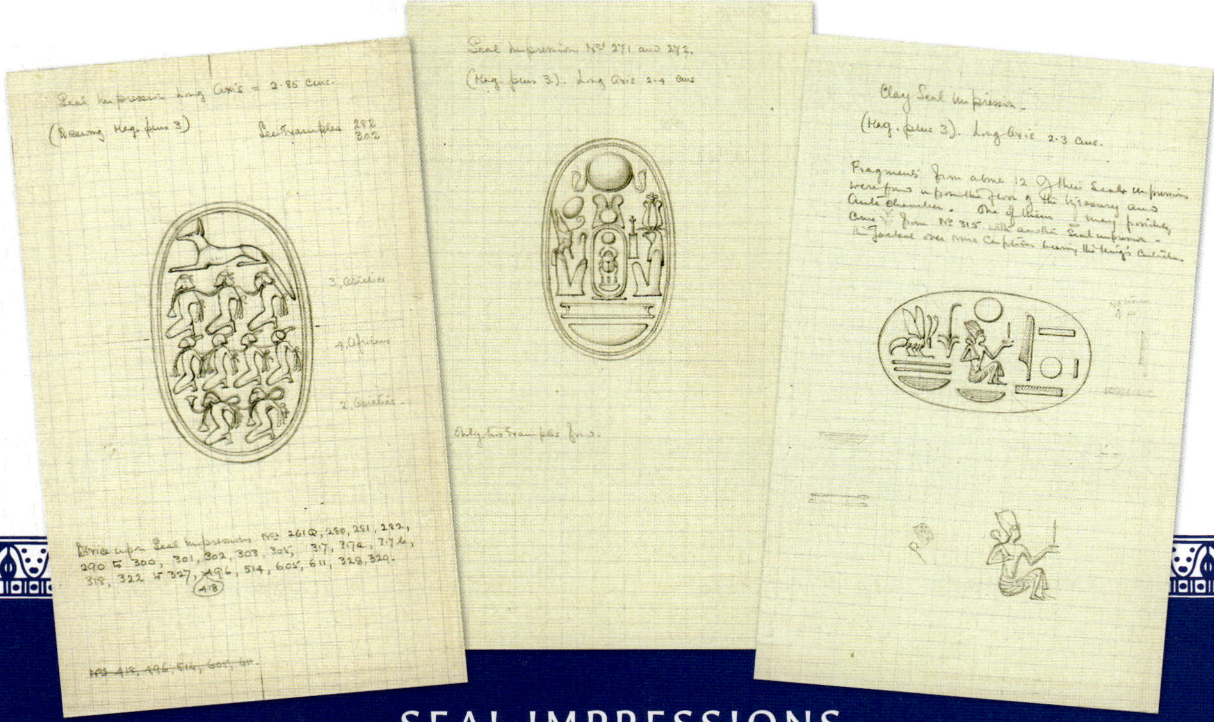

SEAL IMPRESSIONS

The standard method of ensuring that the contents of a room or a tomb would not be tampered with was by sealing the door (or a lid, because the same procedure was used for shrines, boxes and jars). A seal bore the name of the establishment, for example the necropolis, and sometimes of the king or the official who held it. The seals were impressed in the mud plaster while it was still soft. Once the plaster hardened, any intrusion would have been noticed and only the owner of the seal would have been able to re-seal the door or the lid.

"I fear that the Valley of the Kings is now exhausted."

Theodore M Davis 1912

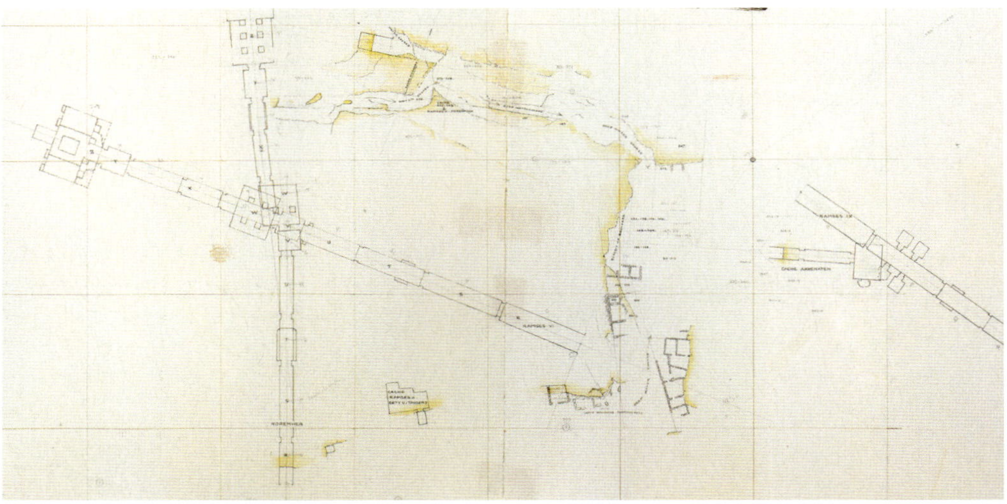

several days in February 1919. The next year, between January and March 1920, he cast his net very wide. He worked in three areas, the beginning of the Valley (between tombs KV 2 of Ramesses IV and KV 9 of Ramesses VI), deep in the Valley near the tomb of Thutmose III (KV 34) and in the small wadi that he had visited in 1917. These were the tactics of a man who was in a hurry.

Carter was back in the same wadi in December 1920. In his excavation journal he indicates that he was encouraged by the situation near the tomb of Ramesses VI where "though there were immense heaps of rubbish from former excavations accumulated on the upper stratum and rock slopes, the ground below had not been attacked since ancient times".

The next season started near the tomb of Merneptah-Siptah (KV 47) in February 1922. But this was a false trail; the signs were not at all auspicious. It is said that by then Lord Carnarvon's enthusiasm was flagging and that Carter offered to finance the next year's excavation himself. Lord Carnarvon eventually agreed to provide funding for another season. This began near the tomb of Ramesses VI on 1 November 1922 and, as Carter notes in his journal, an entrance to a previously unknown tomb was discovered, "in bed rock floor of water-course", almost immediately, on 4 November 1922. The first indication of it was a step cut in the Valley's bedrock and the following day this turned out to belong to a staircase down to a doorway blocked with stones, overlaid with mud plaster and covered with seal impressions. The blocking was only partly uncovered. The seal was that of the necropolis, but no royal names were visible.

Lord Carnarvon was in England and so Carter backfilled the staircase and on 6 November sent him a cable in which he wrote with surprising confidence "At last made wonderful discovery in Valley; a magnificent tomb with seals intact; re-covered same for your arrival; congratulations."

Opposite, above: Howard Carter's copies of seal impressions with a jackal, nine captives and the name of Tutankhamun (Nebkheprure).

Opposite, below: Carter's map of the Eastern part of the Valley of the Kings with a grid that he used to record the location of discoveries.

Above: Mud plaster with seal impressions from the blocking of the first doorway.

THE ANTECHAMBER

26 NOVEMBER 1922

Anticipating an important discovery, Carter summoned Arthur Callender, his trusted lieutenant and close friend, from his house at Armant on 10 November. Lord Carnarvon and Lady Evelyn arrived in Cairo on 20 November, and three days later Carnarvon came to Gurna to stay at Carter's house. On the same day, 23 November, Callender began to clear the debris and boulders, which had been heaped over the entrance in order to protect it from plunderers. It took him only a day to uncover again the descending steps and the sealed doorway (later it was established that this was the first of four sealed doorways in the tomb) partly seen three weeks earlier.

Some of the seal impressions in the lower half of the doorway bore the cartouche of Tutankhamun, identifying whatever might lie behind it as being connected with this king. Worryingly, however, the doorway showed signs of having been re-opened and re-closed, suggesting that the contents might have already been plundered in antiquity.

When the stones blocking the doorway were removed, the space behind it proved to be a descending corridor, entirely filled with rubble, leading westward. The filling was mixed with small objects of various dates and so had to be cleared carefully. These included fragments of wooden boxes bearing the cartouches of Kings Smenkhkare and Tutankhamun, and also a scarab with the name of Thutmose III.

Two days later, on Sunday 26 November at about 2.00 pm, the excavators reached a second sealed doorway that was similar to that at the beginning of the corridor. Once again, some of the seal impressions had the cartouche of Tutankhamun. The excitement of the small party, consisting of Carter, Callender, Lord Carnarvon, Lady Evelyn and the reises (chief workmen) can be easily imagined. A small opening was made in the top left corner of the doorway, which revealed that what lay behind the door was not more debris, but some kind of a room. A candle was inserted into the hole and with this miserable lighting Carter peered inside. There can be no better description of what he saw than what he wrote down in his excavation journal:

"It was sometime before one could see, the hot air escaping caused the candle to flicker, but as soon as one's eyes became accustomed to the glimmer of light the interior of the chamber gradually loomed before one, with its strange and wonderful medley of extraordinary and beautiful objects heaped upon one another.

Opposite: This elaborately designed alabaster cup was the first object found in the Antechamber. On the flowers and buds of the lotus that surround the cup there are kneeling figures holding symbols of "eternal life". The text surrounding the rim is a wish that king Tutankhamun will "spend millions of yeas ... sitting with [his] face to the north wind and [his] eyes beholding beauty".

Above, left: The staircase, consisting of 16 steps, leading to the first of the sealed doorways. The stone slab (top left) reads "433.L.16", the find-number of the tomb. The entwined Cs are part of Lord Carnarvon's crest, but may also be understood as Carter & Carnarvon.

Above, right: A view of the contents of the Antechamber through the iron grille, which was installed in the place of the second sealed doorway.

Entrance

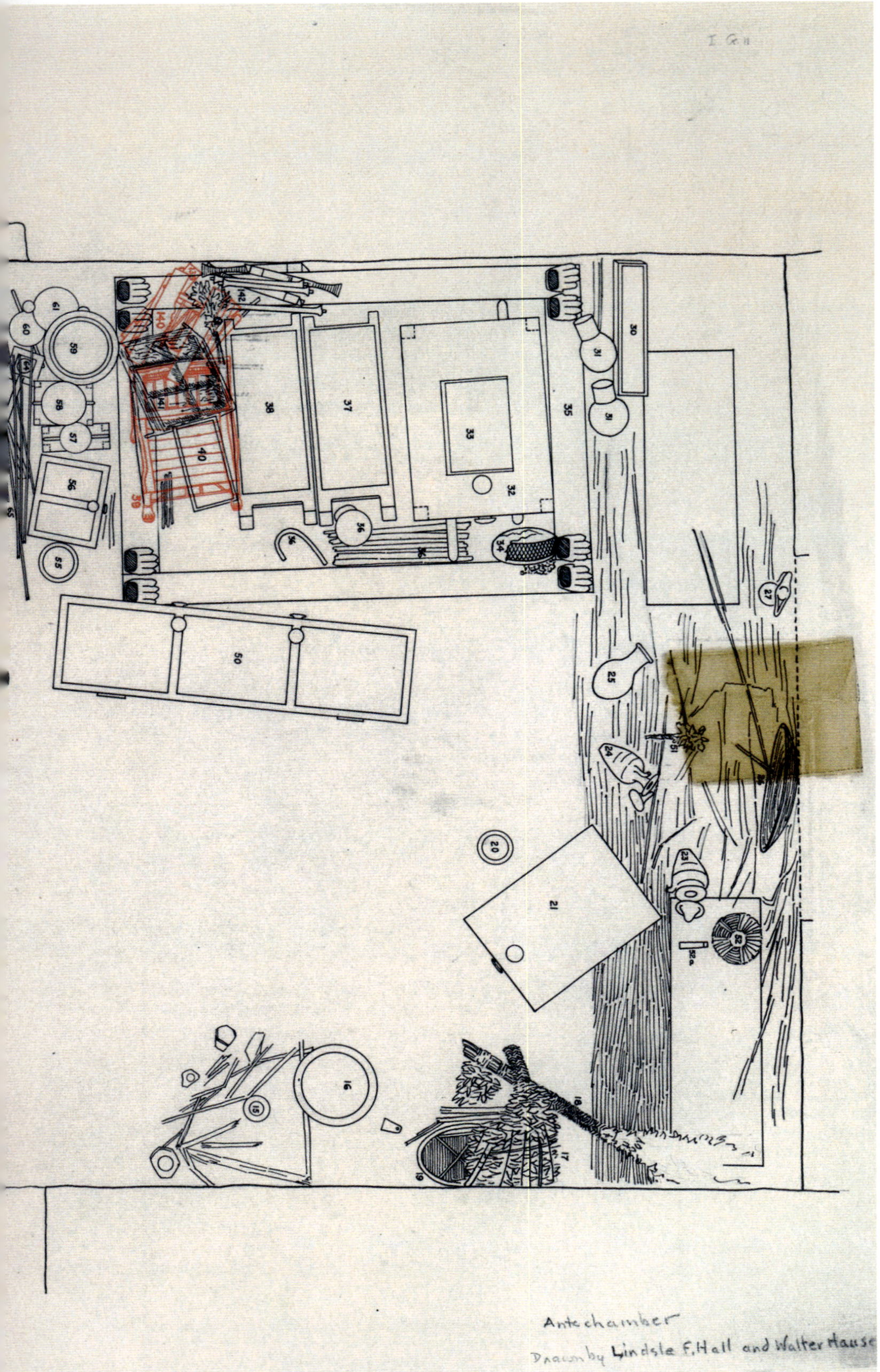

There was naturally short suspense for those present who could not see, when Lord Carnarvon said to me 'Can you see anything'. I replied to him 'Yes, it is wonderful'. I then with precaution made the hole sufficiently large for both of us to see. With the light of an electric torch as well as an additional candle we looked in. Our sensations and astonishment are difficult to describe as the better light revealed to us the marvellous collection of treasures: two strange ebony-black effigies of a King, gold sandalled, bearing staff and mace, loomed out from the cloak of darkness; gilded couches in strange forms, lion-headed, Hathor-headed, and beast infernal; exquisitely painted, inlaid, and ornamental caskets; flowers; alabaster vases, some beautifully executed of lotus and papyrus device; strange black shrines with a gilded monster snake appearing from within; quite ordinary looking white chests; finely carved chairs; a golden inlaid throne; a heap of large curious white oviform boxes; beneath our very eyes, on the threshold, a lovely lotiform wishing-cup in translucent alabaster; stools of all shapes and design, of both common and rare materials; and, lastly a confusion of overturned parts of chariots glinting with gold, peering from amongst which was a mannikin. The first impression of which suggested the property-room of an opera of a vanished civilization. Our sensations were bewildering and full of strange emotion."

Nothing more could be done that day. A note about the discovery was sent to Engelbach, the Chief Inspector of the Antiquities Department, the hole made in the second doorway was re-closed, and the recently installed wooden grille on the tomb's first doorway was locked.

Left: A plan of the Antechamber showing the location of objects in situ, by Walter Hauser and Lindsley Foote Hall.

WONDERFUL THINGS

It appears that the reply to Lord Carnarvon's "Can you see anything?" was a little more prosaic than "Yes, wonderful things", perhaps the most famous words in the history of archaeology. The "authoritative" and more poetic version is quoted on page 96 of the first edition of Howard Carter's *The Tomb of Tut-Ankh-Amen*, but may have been "edited" into the text by Arthur Mace. In his journal, Carter simply says "Yes, it is wonderful".

Above: An alabaster (calcite), ornamental unguent jar in the form symbolising the "union of Upper and Lower Egypt".

Opposite, above: A view of the southern part of the Antechamber looking to the left from the second doorway.

Opposite, below left: Objects piled up against the western wall of the Antechamber, seen from the second doorway.

Opposite, below right: The northern end of the Antechamber, seen from the second doorway and looking to the right. The sealed entrance to the Burial Chamber is between the two statues of Tutankhamun.

5,398 items were found in Tutankhamun's tomb and it took Howard Carter over ten years to catalogue it all

THE TOMB

The Valley of the Kings has several branches and Tutankhamun's tomb (numbered KV 62, with KV standing for Kings' Valley) is situated in the main, or East, Valley. The tombs further into the Valley are chronologically earlier, so Tutankhamun's neighbours are several Ramessid kings (of the 19th and 20th Dynasties, 1295–1069 BC). Significantly, there are also tombs KV 55, of a member of the Amarna royal family, possibly King Akhenaten himself, and KV 57, of Haremhab, in this area.

Opposite: The entrance to the tomb of Tutankhamun (right of centre foreground), and those of Ramesses VI (KV 9, behind), Amenmesse (KV 10, lower left) and Ramesses III (KV 11, above KV10).

Above: The approach to the tomb from the north, with the hill of El-Gurn in the background.

The subterranean royal tombs in the Valley of the Kings are all of the pharaohs of the New Kingdom, after about 1525 BC. They are cut deep into the rather poor-quality limestone rock characteristic of the Theban area and have no obvious adjoining buildings outside the long syrinx (gallery) itself. Their plans consist of a series of rooms and corridors strung like beads along straight descending lines. Tuthmosid tombs (of the 18th dynasty), after a straight beginning, tend to veer to the left ("bent" tombs) and so follow the traditional orientation of Egyptian royal funerary monuments. Ramessid tombs (of the 19th and 20th dynasties) maintain the straight line.

The small size of Tutankhamun's tomb – the overall area of the rooms, excluding the Staircase, the Descending Passage and the doorways, is only about 82.5 sq m (888 sq ft) – and its simple and unusual plan (only four rooms) have led to the

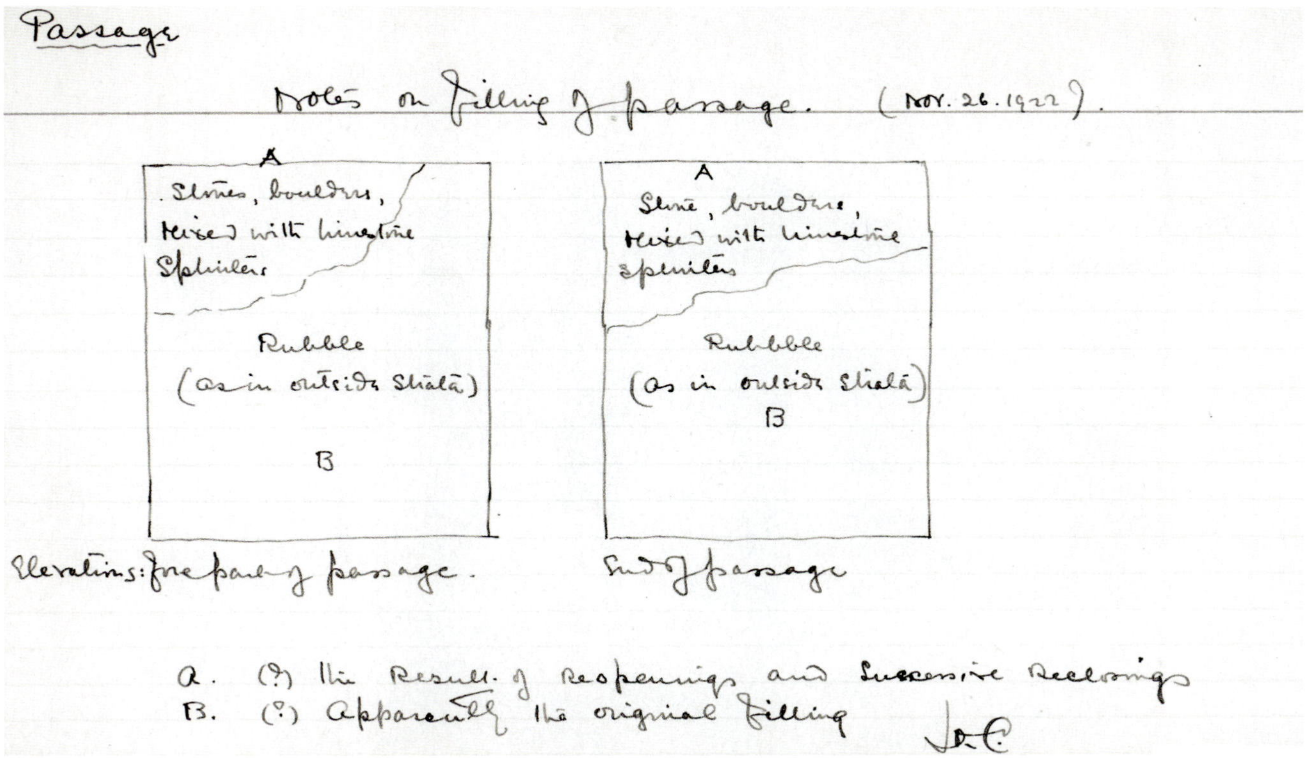

WHY DID THE TOMB REMAIN UNDETECTED?

Two factors enhanced the tomb's chances of remaining undetected and largely unplundered. On his plan of the area Howard Carter indicates a "deep water course" immediately over the entrance to the tomb. Rains occurred infrequently but would have carried and deposited sand and rubble which would have masked the entrance. Furthermore, débris and the huts of workmen engaged in the excavation of the tomb of Ramesses VI nearly 200 years later would have completely concealed any traces of the entrance to the tomb.

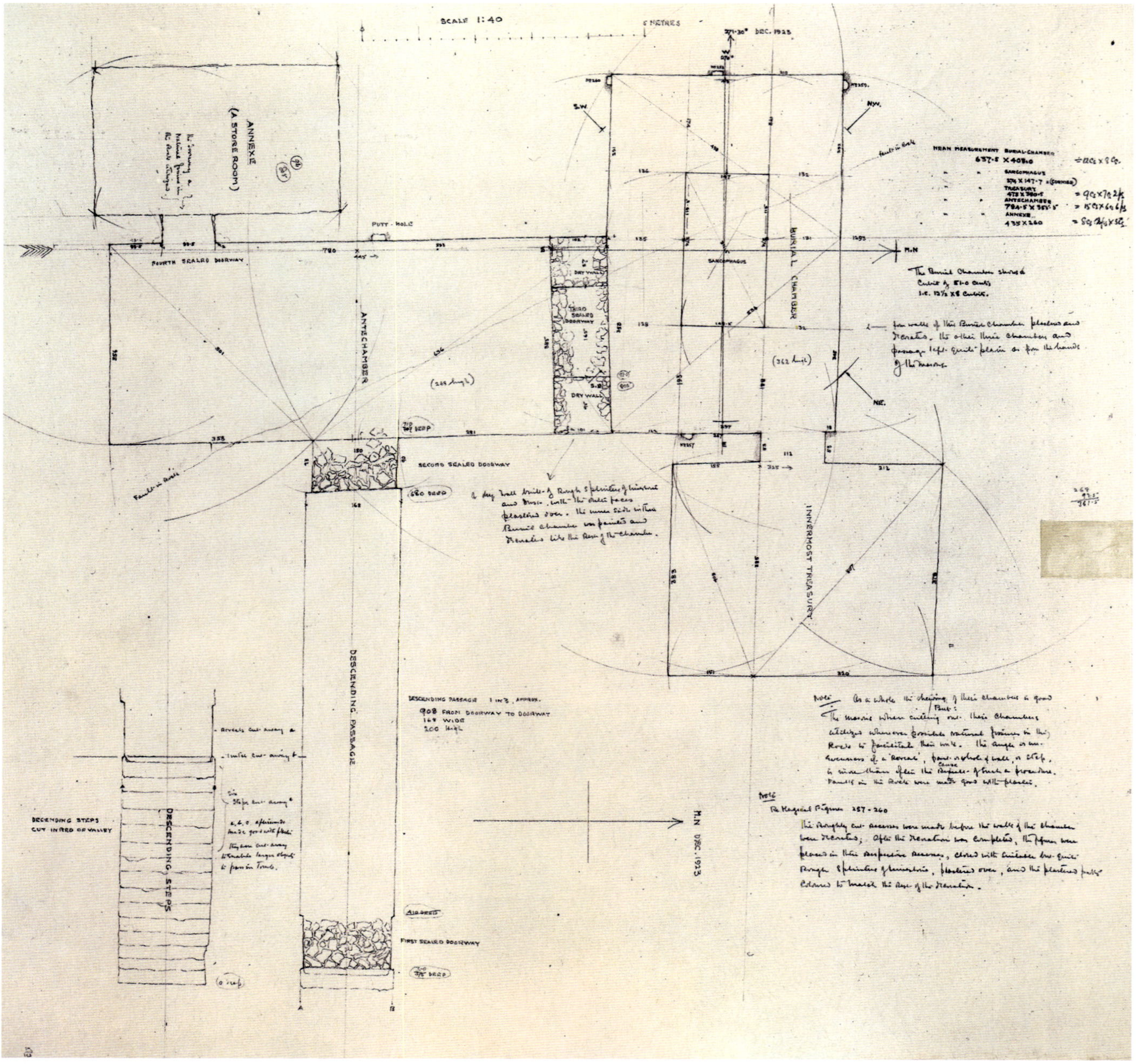

Opposite: Howard Carter's notes on the traces of the robbers' tunnel in the filling of the Descending Passage.
Above: Howard Carter's plan of the tomb with detailed measurements and orientation.

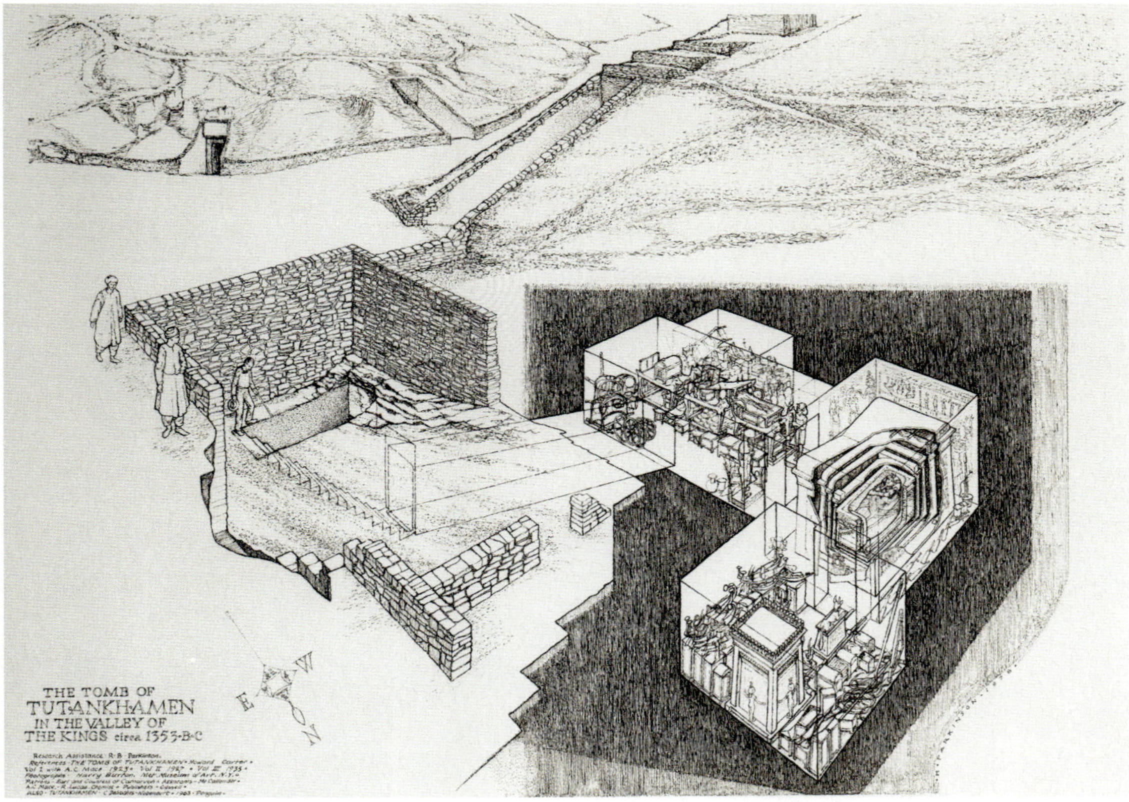

Above: An axonometric plan of the tomb.

Left: The entrance to the tomb, seen from the north.

Opposite: A list of boxes with the objects that were removed from Tutankhamun's tomb on 1 April 1924.

THE ROBBERIES

There are four indications that Tutankhamun's tomb did not completely avoid the attention of ancient tomb robbers: (1) the re-sealed doorways, (2) the filling of the Descending Passage with rubble in order to prevent, unsuccessfully, further attacks by robbers, (3) the confusion in which the contents of the tomb were found, and (4) the damage done to some of the items. The suggestion that some valuable objects, such as jewellery, are missing is more difficult to prove. All the doorways were broken through and, with the exception of the Annexe, re-sealed. The doorway at the bottom of the entrance staircase showed signs of being opened and re-sealed twice. The situation inside the tomb is obscured by the fact that the funerary equipment seems to have been deposited in a hurry in a very confined space. Some items were found in a state which suggested hasty examination and ransacking. Interestingly, it appears that metal which could be easily disposed of, such as bronze, may often have been taken in preference to gold. Some of these thefts and acts of damage could, of course, have taken place before the objects were deposited in the tomb, for example while in storage before the funeral. The robberies probably took place only a few years after Tutankhamun's burial.

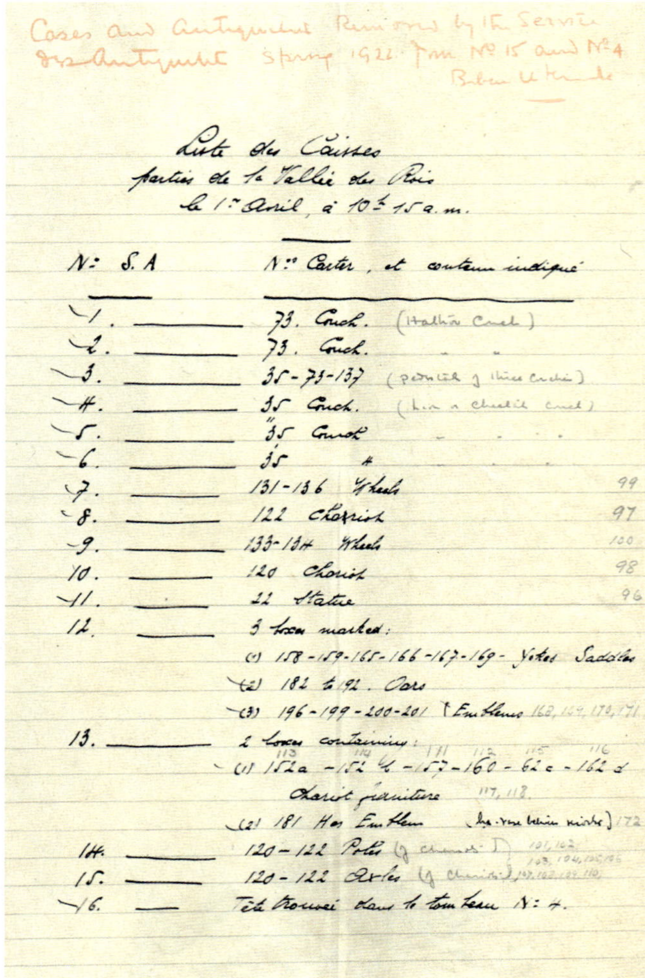

Liste des Caisses
parties de la Vallée des Rois
le 1er Avril, à 10h 15 a.m.

N° S. A	N° Carter, et contenu indiqué
1.	73. Couch. (Hathor Couch)
2.	73. Couch.
3.	35-73-137
4.	35 Couch.
5.	35 Couch
6.	35 "
7.	131-136 Wheels 99
8.	122 Chariot 97
9.	133-134 Wheels 100
10.	120 Chariot 98
11.	22 Statue 96
12.	3 boxes marked: (1) 158-159-165-166-167-169- Yokes Saddles (2) 182 to 192. Oars (3) 196-199-200-201 & Emblems 168, 169, 170, 171
13.	2 boxes containing: (1) 152a -152 b -157-160 - 62c - 162 d Chariot furniture 117, 118. (2) 181 Hor Emblem 172
14.	120-122 Poles
15.	120-122 Axles
16.	Tête trouvée dans le tombeau N: 4.

suggestion that it was originally planned as a non-royal tomb which was, after the King's premature death, hastily converted for royal use. This, however, is far from certain. The plan is not unlike that of the tombs of Tutankhamun's successor Aye (KV 23) and, to a lesser degree, of Aye's successor Haremhab (KV 57). It probably represents a post-Amarna development in royal funerary architecture. To complete such a tomb in the time which elapsed between Tutankhamun's death and his funeral would not have been beyond the capabilities of Egyptian stonemasons.

Sixteen steps cut into the bedrock descend at an angle of about 30 degrees from the floor of the Valley westward to the first sealed doorway. Beyond it there is a Descending Passage, 9.08 m (29 ft 27 in) long, 1.68 m (5 ft 6 in) wide and 2 m (6 ft 6 in) high. This was found completely filled with sand and rubble, probably following the first robbery.

At the end of the Descending Passage is a doorway leading into the tomb's first room, the so-called Antechamber, which is some 27.5 sq m (296 sq ft) in size and 2.68 m (8 ft 9 in) high. The cutting of this room, as everywhere in the tomb, is somewhat irregular. Its floor is only 7.1 m (23 ft 4 in) below that of the Valley. The room served as the tomb's main storage area. In this function it was supplemented by another, smaller, room (the so-called Annexe, of some 11.5 sq m/124 sq ft) connected with it by a doorway in its south-west corner.

A third doorway, in the northern wall, linked the Antechamber with the Burial Chamber, which is about 25.5 sq m (274 sq ft) in size and 3.62 m (nearly 12 ft) high. The Antechamber and the Burial Chamber were created out of one L-shaped room by a dry masonry partition wall with a doorway but the floor of the Burial Chamber is 0.94 m (just over 3 ft) lower than that of the Antechamber. The doorway leading into the fourth room, the so-called Treasury (about 18 sq m/194 sq ft), was not sealed. The main purpose of this room was to house Tutankhamun's internal organs removed during mummification, the foetuses of his still-born children, and some of the ritual objects closely connected with the burial.

THE EXCAVATORS

Howard Carter, the excavator, and Lord Carnarvon, the sponsor who financed the excavation, were worlds apart in background, education, social standing and wealth, yet they both possessed that indescribable something that made them ideal partners in archaeology. Each of them probably saw qualities in the other that he admired, but lacked himself. Lord Carnarvon's death on 5 April 1923, only a little more than four months after the opening of Tutankhamun's tomb, must have been an enormous blow for Carter, yet the entry in his pocket diary simply says "Ld. C. died 2 am".

Above: The team (from left): Callender, Mace, Burton, Carter, Gardiner and Lucas.

Opposite, clockwise from top left: Lord Carnarvon who financed Howard Carter's excavations; Carter and an Egyptian assistant bringing one of the couches out of the tomb; the contribution of Egyptian reises (foremen) and workmen to the success of the project was invaluable; Mace (standing) and Lucas at work in the "laboratory" (the tomb of Sety II).

After Lord Carnarvon's death, the excavation continued to be financed by his widow, Almina, Countess of Carnarvon. There was no division of the discovered objects between the Antiquities Service and the excavators, but in 1930 she received £36,000 in compensation for excavation costs from the Egyptian government. The work that began in November 1922 was concluded after ten seasons in February 1932.

From all accounts, Howard Carter was quick-tempered, occasionally tactless, with a penchant for showmanship, and bitterly resentful of those who regarded themselves as his social superiors because of their birth or education. He was not easy to get on with by any means. He was a man of his time, with many of the prejudices of the period, yet he was also remarkably modern in his warm relationship with Egyptian workmen and his stubborn defence of principles whatever the pressure. At best he was tolerated but often shunned by the British academic community and he, in his turn, did not make any overt attempt to ingratiate himself.

It was probably inevitable that only Burton and Lucas, both entrusted with specialised tasks, lasted the whole excavation. It was largely due to Carter's determination that he saw the recording of the tomb through. Carter was the man for the task.

A considerable contribution to the work in Tutankhamun's tomb was made by American Egyptologists. Carter's friendship with the members of the Egyptian Expedition of the Metropolitan Museum of Art and the generous support received from the Curator of Egyptian Art, Albert Lythgoe, were crucial when Carter was assembling his team. In fact, the work of Mace, Burton, Hall and Hauser was financed by the Egyptian Expedition of the Metropolitan Museum of Art.

THE "CURSE OF THE PHARAOH"

Texts in some early Egyptian tombs contained threats against those who would damage the burial, but nothing of the kind was found in the tomb of Tutankhamun. The main inspiration for the legend of Tutankhamun's curse which brought misfortune upon those who disturbed the pharaoh's peace was the death of Lord Carnarvon from blood poisoning and pneumonia on 5 April 1923, at the age of 56, less than five months after the opening of the tomb. Several other incidents were linked with it. A cobra devoured a canary given to Carter by Lord Carnarvon's daughter, Lady Evelyn, two days before the opening of the tomb (either as a pet bird or in order to test the atmosphere in the tomb). Electric lights went off in Cairo and Lord Carnarvon's favourite dog died at Highclere at the same time as its master. Some of those closely involved in the excavation died early: Mace at 53 in 1928, Callender at 60 in 1936, Burton at 60 in 1940, Carter at 64 in 1939, but others lived to a ripe old age: Breasted died at 70 in 1935, Lucas at 78 in 1945, Derry at 86 in 1961 (as the man who examined Tutankhamun's mummy he should have been first in line for the curse). The notion of the curse may have started as a joke by the Egyptologist Arthur Weigall; he himself died at 53 in 1934. There is no scientific support for the legend.

Left: Carter (left), Callender and an Egyptian assistant preparing one of the "guardian statues" for transport.

Above: Professor and Mrs Newberry restoring the pall that was found draped over a wooden framework over the inner shrines.

THE TEAM

CALLENDER, ARTHUR ROBERT (1876-1936)
"Callender continued clearing and putting to rights the magazine, and also prepared a platform beside the sarcophagus for Burton to photograph from."
Carter's journal, 1 February 1925
A retired engineer and manager of the Egyptian branch railways who lived at Armant, Callender looked after the practical aspects of the excavation. He was one of Carter's closest friends, but their relationship was stormy and came to an end in the spring of 1925.

MACE, ARTHUR CRUTTENDEN (1874-1928)
"Mace commenced preservation of couch No. 45 - lion headed."
Carter's journal, 19 November 1923
A British archaeologist who worked with various American missions in Egypt, Mace was appointed Assistant Curator in the Metropolitan Museum of Art in New York in 1909 and Associate Curator in 1922. He took part in the 1922-3 and 1923-4 excavation seasons, but had to retire due to ill health. He co-authoured the first volume of *The Tomb of Tut-Ankh-Amen.*

BURTON, HARRY (1879-1940)
A British archaeologist and photographer who was responsible for photographic documentation.

LUCAS, ALFRED (1867-1945)
"Saw Lucas, Director of Chemical Dept. of Egyptian Government, and he offered services for winter."
Carter's journal, 7 December 1922
A chemist employed by the Egyptian Government and the Antiquities Service, Lucas was in charge of the restoration and conservation of objects.

GARDINER, (SIR) ALAN HENDERSON (1879-1963)
"Lord C. arranged with Gardiner in England to look after philological end of work."
Carter's journal, 18 December 1922
An Egyptologist specialising in the ancient Egyptian language, Gardiner copied many inscriptions on objects in the tomb.

Reis Ahmed, Reis Hussein Abou Omar and other anonymous Egyptian workmen.

THE SPECIALISTS AND ASSISTANTS

Most of these came to help with specialised tasks or provided reports without participating in the excavation.

BREASTED, JAMES HENRY (1865-1935)
Professor of Egyptology and Oriental History, University of Chicago, and founder of the Oriental Institute, Chicago, Breasted helped to record the seal impressions in the tomb in the 1922-3 season of work.

NEWBERRY, PERCY EDWARD (1868-1949)
An Egyptologist and botanist who helped with the botanical specimens and some inscriptions during the 1923-4 season.

NEWBERRY, ESSIE WINIFRED (1878-1953)
The wife of Professor Newberry, she undertook the conservation of the pall draped over the second shrine during the 1923-4 season.
DERRY, DOUGLAS ERITH (1874-1961)
An anatomist who was the first to examine Tutankhamun's mummy.

BETHELL, (HON.) RICHARD (1883-1929)
A collector and member of the committee of the Egypt Exploration Society who worked as Carter's assistant during the 1923-4 season.

HALL, LINDSLEY FOOTE (1883-1969), draughtsman
HAUSER, WALTER (1893-1959), archaeologist and architect
Both were American and working with the Egyptian Expedition of the Metropolitan Museum of Art, New York. They prepared the plans showing the arrangement of objects in the Antechamber.

RECORDING THE CONTENTS OF TUTANKHAMUN'S TOMB

The astonishing extent of the discovery and the confusion in which the material was found presented huge problems when records were made. Tutankhamun's tomb contained at least 5,398 objects. This calculation is on the low side. For example, a chariot dismantled into dozens of pieces was counted as one object.

Fortunately, Carter was an experienced archaeologist and his team, although remarkably small by modern standards, included first-class specialists. His recording techniques were a natural development of what he had learnt and used during his earlier archaeological career. They were relatively simple, but effective. Most importantly, Carter's dogged perseverance in the face of all the difficulties and interruptions achieved what seemed like an almost impossible task: a complete archaeological record of the tomb and its contents.

The record of the objects found in the tomb consists essentially of two elements: object cards (there are about 3,150 of them) and black-and-white photographs (about 1,850). Carter assigned numbers ranging from 1 to 620 to the objects but many of these are further subdivided, for example when referring to the contents of a box. Each object thus has its unique identifier to which all the other records refer. A handwritten record of each item was then made on one or more index cards measuring about 20.5 by 12.5 cm (8.25 x 5.25 in). The recording was carried out by Carter himself or, during the early stages of work, by Arthur Mace. The notes on the cards included each object's position in the tomb, its measurements, material and main physical characteristics, and, when necessary, included a sketch.

Opposite: Find 23, the painted pottery jar that was found in the Antechamber, in detail.

Above: Objects found in front of the sealed doorway to the Burial Chamber. These included a pottery jar (seen next to the pedestal of the statue on the right) that was numbered as find 23.

Inscriptions were copied on to the cards or on small sheets of paper attached to the cards by Carter himself or A H Gardiner. Alfred Lucas added notes on any conservation or restoration measures undertaken on site. In addition to the notes which he made on object cards, Lucas also maintained his own detailed records which included a register of samples and notes on the examination of materials.

Howard Carter kept a journal in which he described in varying detail the daily activities in the tomb. It only rarely adds significantly to the other records, with the exception of the examination of the King's mummy and objects found on it. For the first three seasons (1922–5) there are also Carter's personal pocket diaries although these contain hardly any archaeological information.

RECORD CARDS AND PHOTOGRAPHS

The relationship between hand-written cards and photographs can be seen in the record of a tall, painted, pottery jar (left), that was found in the Antechamber and numbered 23. The card shown above was made by Arthur Mace and includes a sketch of the jar; a second card (not shown) has notes, made by Alfred Lucas, on the repair of the object. Burton's first photograph (left) shows the objects as they were found near the sealed doorway of the Burial Chamber, with the jar close to the pedestal of one of the "guardian statues".

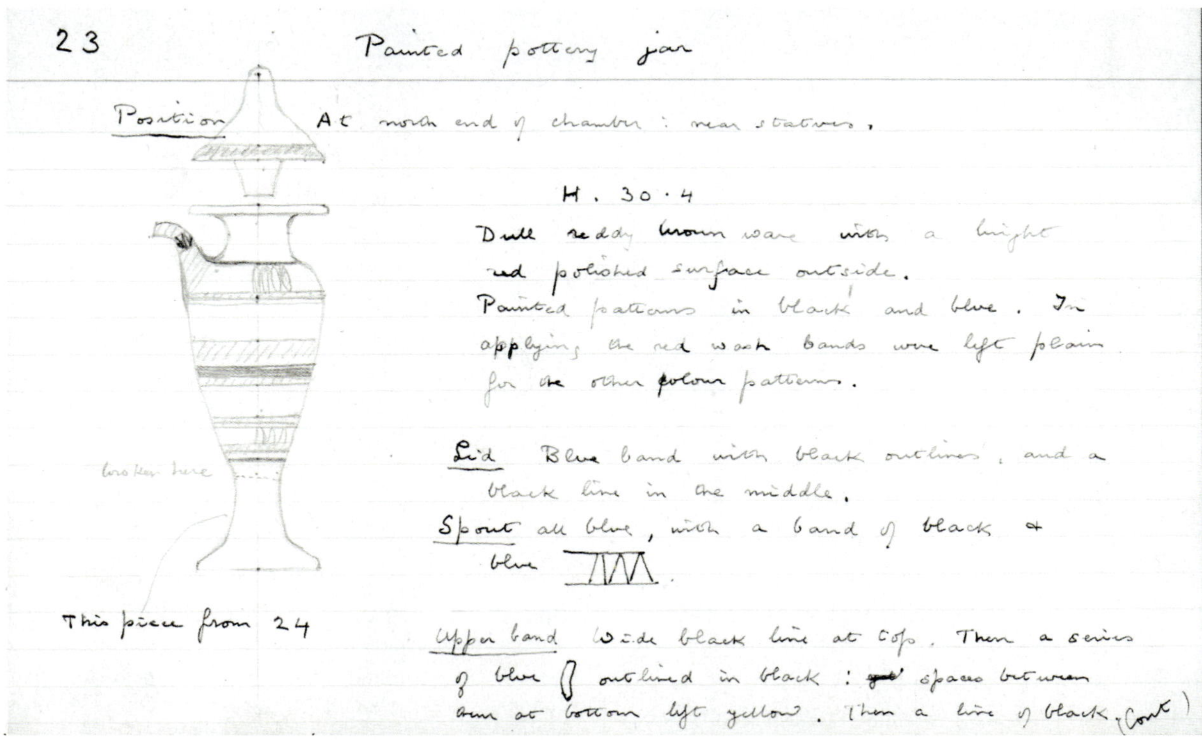
23 Painted pottery jar

Position At north end of chamber: near statues.

H. 30·4

Dull reddy brown ware with a bright red polished surface outside.
Painted patterns in black and blue. In applying the red wash bands were left plain for the other colour patterns.

Lid Blue band with black outlines, and a black line in the middle.
Spout all blue, with a band of black & blue.

broken here

This piece from 24

Upper band Wide black line at top. Then a series of blue outlined in black: spaces between them at bottom left yellow. Then a line of black (Cont)

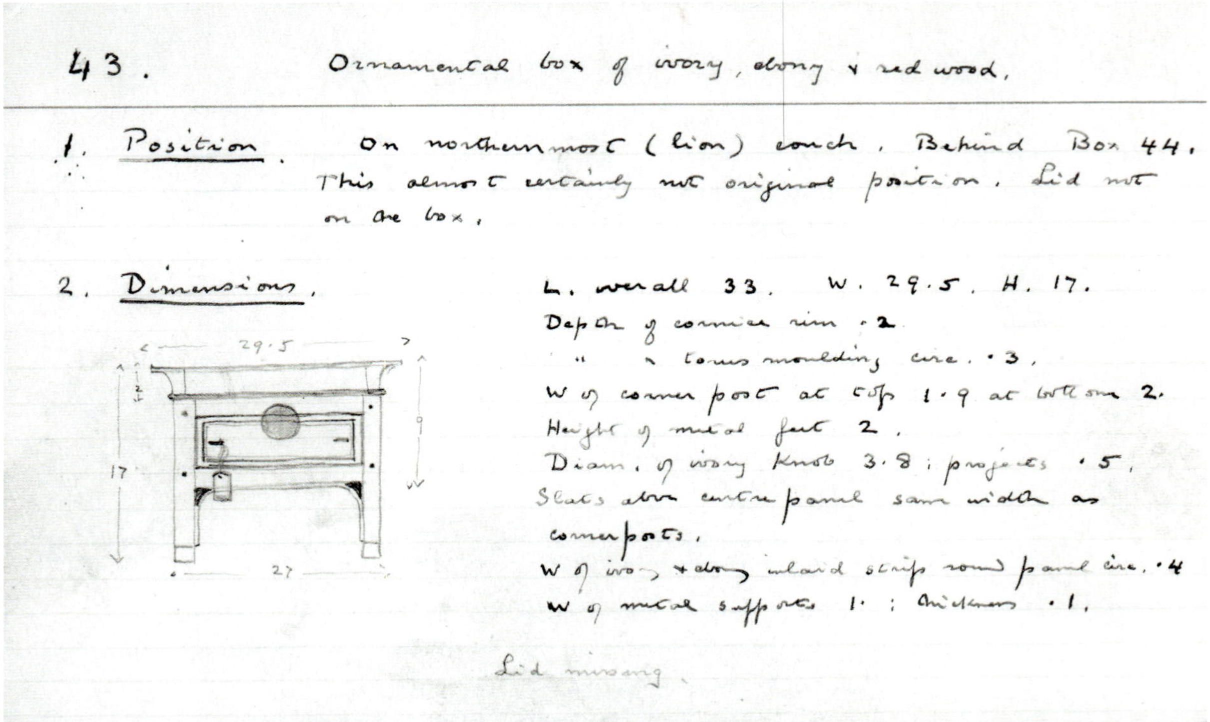

43. Ornamental box of ivory, ebony & red wood.

1. Position. On northernmost (lion) couch. Behind Box 44. This almost certainly not original position. Lid not on the box.

2. Dimensions. L. overall 33. W. 29.5. H. 17.
Depth of cornice rim ·2
" " torus moulding circ. ·3.
W of corner post at top 1·9 at bottom 2.
Height of metal feet 2.
Diam. of ivory knob 3.8; projects ·5.
Slats above centre panel same width as cornerposts.
W of ivory & ebony inlaid strip round panel circ. ·4
W of metal supports 1· ; thickness ·1.

Lid missing.

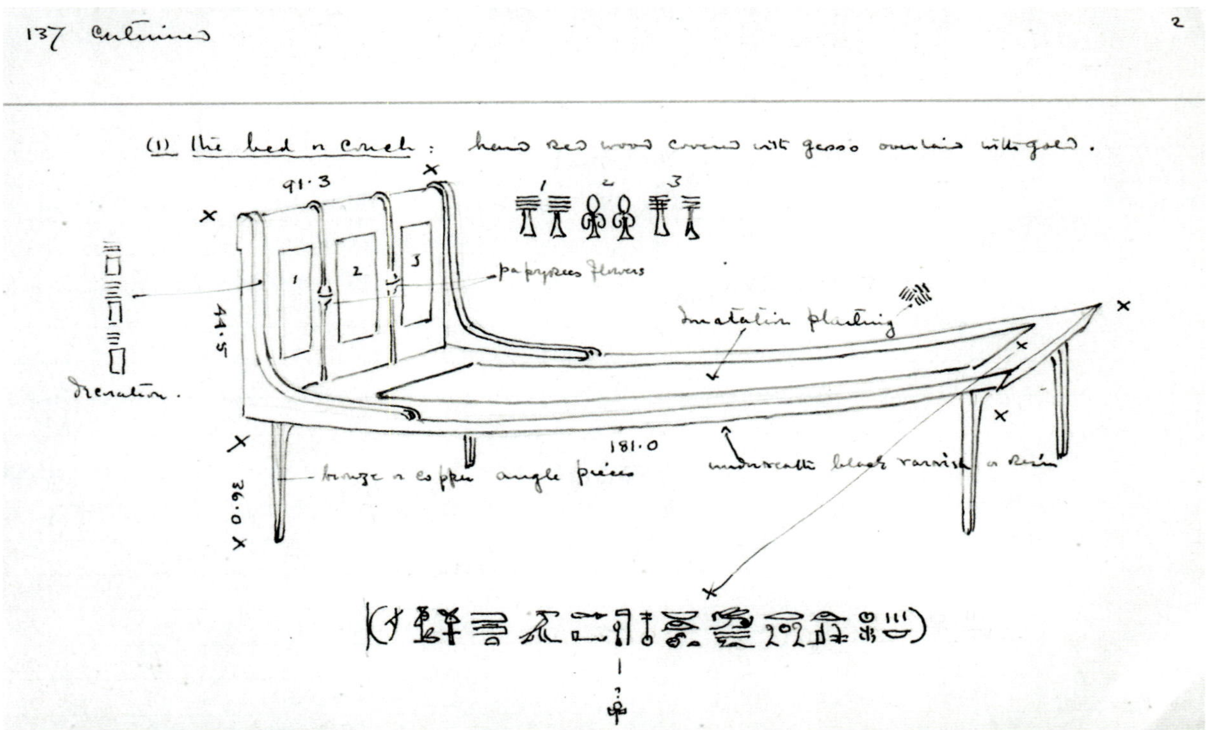

137 continued 2

(1) The bed or couch: hard red wood covered with gesso overlaid with gold.

Above: Record cards for objects 43 (ornamental box), by Arthur Mace, and 137 (hippopotamus couch), by Howard Carter.

261 ANUBIS

POSITION: Placed in centre of chamber, partially blocking the doorway, facing west. Ends of carrying-poles of shrine protruding into the Burial Chamber (see note attached).

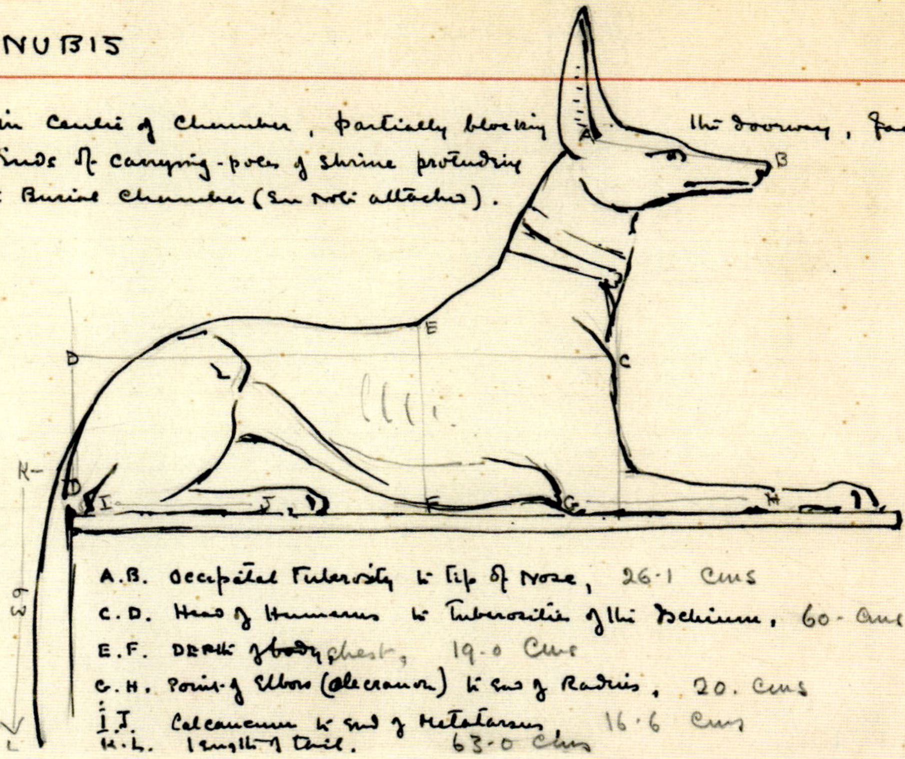

DIMENSIONS: Anubis Jackal

A.B. Occipital Tuberosity to tip of nose, 26·1 Cms

C.D. Head of Humerus to Tuberosities of the Ischium, 60· Cms

E.F. Depth of ~~body~~ chest, 19·0 Cms

G.H. Point of Elbow (Olecranon) to end of Radius, 20. Cms

I.J. Calcaneum to end of Metatarsus, 16·6 Cms

K.L. Length of tail. 63·0 Cms

(261 Continued) (2)

DESCRIPTION: A recumbent figure of the Jackal Anubis, carved of wood, thinly coated with gesso, and painted black.
The pectination of the interior of the ears, the collar, and the scarf, gilt.
The eyes and eye-brows inlaid with gold, the eye-balls of calcite, the pupils of obsidian; the corners of the eye-balls slightly tinged red.
The toe-nails of silver, blackened by corrosion.
The legs and feet of the jackal are pegged to a flat board, gilt, measuring 91·5 × 25·0, cms; this board slides on to the top of the pylonic shrine, to which it acts as a lid.

Between the fore-paws was an ivory palette (see 262).

(261 A) Was covered with a linen shirt (see note 261A)

(261 B) Under shirt a muslin like covering (see note 261B).

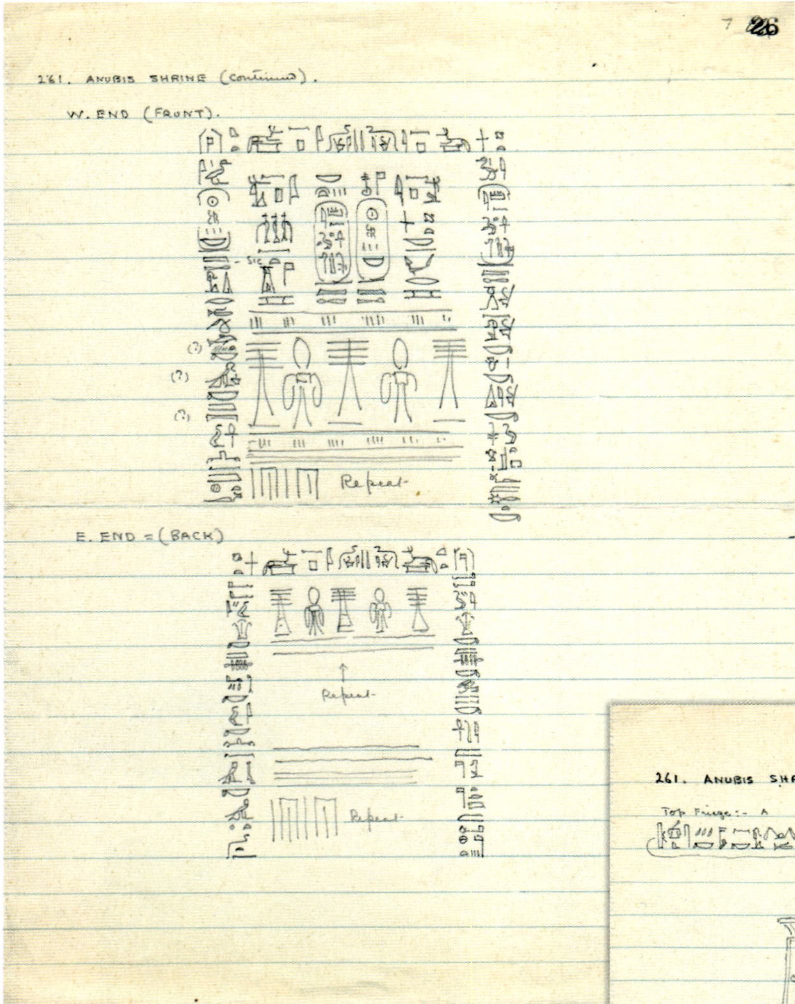

261. ANUBIS SHRINE (continued).

W. END (FRONT).

Repeat.

E. END = (BACK)

Repeat.

Repeat.

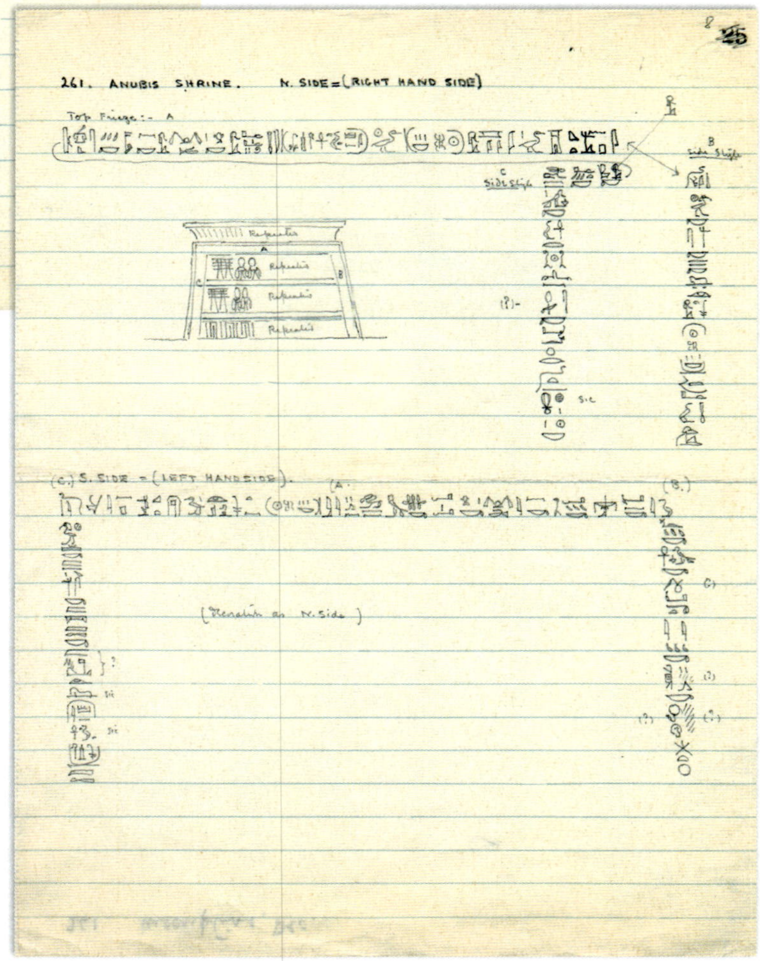

261. ANUBIS SHRINE. N. SIDE = (RIGHT HAND SIDE)

Top Frieze :- A

(C.) S. SIDE = (LEFT HAND SIDE).

(Remainder as N. Side)

Opposite, above and right: Howard Carter's record cards for object 261, a portable image of Anubis as a jackal, on a shrine with carrying poles.

Plans of the four rooms showing how objects were deposited in them were made, some of them by L F Hall and W Hauser. Detailed drawings of a small number of items, especially chariot parts, were made by Carter. Additional information on some aspects of the discovery, such as botany and materials, was provided by several specialists and some of them prepared separate reports.

Harry Burton's photographs complete the descriptions of objects on the cards and provide information on the context in which they were found.

Much of the recording took place in the tomb but some was done in the "laboratory", a workroom and storeroom set up in KV 15, the tomb of Sety II.

Howard Carter's excavation records and Harry Burton's photographs are now in the Archive of the Griffith Institute in Oxford.

Below: Most of the recording was made by Howard Carter himself, with frequent interruptions by visitors, pressmen, and many other tasks connected with the running of the excavation.

Opposite: A richly decorated box with Tutankhamun and his queen in a hunting scene and various animal and floral motifs. These pictures are inlaid in ivory, ebony, faience, glass and alabaster.

TUTANKHAMUN: ANATOMY OF AN EXCAVATION WEBSITE

(http://www.griffith.ox.ac.uk/discoveringtut/)

All Carter's excavation records and one set of the original glass negatives made by Harry Burton are kept in the Archive of the Griffith Institute in Oxford. When the state of publication of the material was assessed in the late 1990s, it was established that the progress made until then was not satisfactory and so it was decided to make all the excavation records available on the Griffith Institute's website. The project began in 2000 and still continues. The director of the project is Jaromir Malek, while the computing expertise is provided by Jonathan Moffett. Other members, especially Elizabeth Fleming, Diana Magee, Alison Hobby, Kent Rawlinson, Sue Hutchison, Lindsay Allen and others, have been involved in the scanning, the preparation of the transcript and editing. The written material is presented in transcripts as well as scans of the original records and much emphasis is placed on the ability to search the records in the database quickly. The site is a huge success: in 2005 the number of pages consulted every month varied between 1 and 1.5 million.

HARRY BURTON

Photographing objects in situ, as well as those removed to the "laboratory" (KV 15, the tomb of Sety II) was the task of Harry Burton. His photographs combine information and artistry and are among the most attractive archaeological images ever taken. They have contributed, more than anything else, to the public perception of the discovery of Tutankhamun's tomb. Harry Burton is the best-known archaeological photographer of all times.

Above: Harry Burton (1879–1940), a supreme master of archaeological photography.
Opposite: The desolation of the Valley of the Kings.

Harry Burton spent a total of eight years photographing Tutankhamun's tombs and it's artefacts

Harry Burton was born in Stamford in Lincolnshire on 13 September 1879. The young Burton became a secretary to the art historian Robert Henry Hobart Cust and stayed with him in Florence where he began to take photographs. In this he proved to be remarkably talented. It was there that he also met the American archaeologist Theodore M Davis. Although Burton had no archaeological experience, Davis asked him to come and work at his excavations at Thebes in 1910.

Theodore Davis stopped excavating in Egypt shortly before the First World War, but by then Burton's double archaeological and photographic career was truly launched. In 1914, he was invited by Albert M Lythgoe, the Curator of Egyptian Art in the Metropolitan Museum of Art in New York, to join their Egyptian Expedition as a photographer. His task was to provide a pictorial record of the most important ancient Egyptian monuments in the area of the Theban necropolis, on the west bank opposite modern Luxor. Among Egyptologists, these pictures are now known as "MMA photographs".

In December 1922, Lythgoe "lent" Burton to Carter in order to document the discovery of the tomb of Tutankhamun. Both Carter and Lord Carnarvon were competent photographers themselves, but the task required professional skills. Burton combined his involvement in Tutankhamun's tomb with continued photographic work for the Egyptian Expedition. He stayed with Carter throughout the whole campaign. He died in Asyut on 27 June 1940 and was buried there.

Burton's photographs are distinguished by perfection of composition, even quality of lighting, fine detail of the subject matter and the supreme understanding of what an archaeologist requires from photographs taken during an excavation. It probably is not too fanciful to trace the first three qualities back to the time when Burton photographed Florentine paintings. His experience as a field archaeologist explains the last feature.

Harry Burton's images of Tutankhamun's treasures were taken on large glass plate negatives measuring approx. 18 x 24 cm (approx. 7 x 9.5 in), which were then contact-printed.

Above: Three of Harry Burton's own prints of photographs of Tutankhamun's "throne". They show one of the two lion heads from the front of the "throne", four cobras with sun discs from the rear of the back and Queen Ankhesenamun anointing seated Tutankhamun, also from the back of the "throne".

Left: An alabaster perfume or unguent vase with a symbol of the "union of Upper and Lower Egypt" and the names of Tutankhamun and Queen Ankhesenamun. It was found in the Burial Chamber.

BURTON'S METHOD

If any criticism can be levelled at Harry Burton's method of photographing, it is that, by modern standards, his photographs are not always sufficiently rigidly systematic. His method can be demonstrated by the throne, 91 in Carter's numbering. It was found under the Amemet couch in the Antechamber and was photographed several times in situ in general views without numbers (far right) as well as with numbers (right), but the views are not identical. Almost all objects were also photographed individually with their numbers.

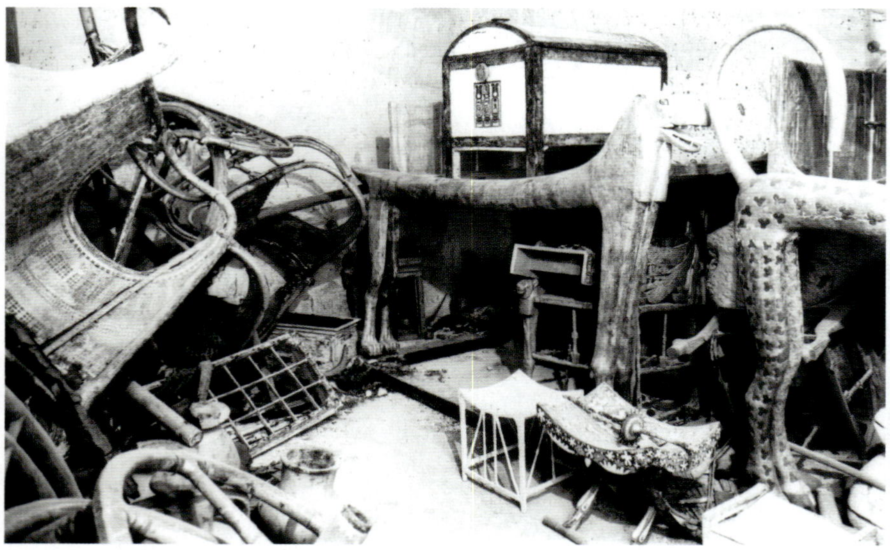

Burton also experimented with colour photography (his colour plates are now apparently lost) and cinematography, but black-and-white photographs remained his favourite medium. During his career, Burton often had to do with the light reflected into tombs by large mirrors, but he used multiple electric floodlights for photography in the tomb of Tutankhamun. Tomb KV 55, close to the tomb of Tutankhamun, was used as his darkroom.

There are two sets of Burton's glass negatives, one in the Griffith Institute in Oxford, the other in the Metropolitan Museum of Art in New York. In theory, the two sets are identical, but some of the pictures show slight variations. The Griffith Institute set consists of some 1,250 glass plate negatives and some 600 additional images. The Institute also possesses ten albums with prints, which were almost certainly made by Burton himself. This is important because some manipulation of the image took place during printing and so these photographs can be regarded as the ultimate Burton images of Tutankhamun's tomb.

Above, top: A group of objects photographed by Harry Burton with number labels. The throne under the couch is numbered 91.

Above, left: The same group of objects taken without number labels. Note the throne (91) under the Amemet couch.

Above, right: The Anubis jackal, the deity of the necropolis, on a portable shrine found in the Treasury.

28
26

OPENING THE BURIAL CHAMBER

FRIDAY, 16 FEBRUARY 1923

In less than three months, after the first glimpse of the "wonderful things" in the Antechamber, the room was emptied. Only the two statues of Tutankhamun still stood flanking the third sealed doorway in the north wall. There was no way of knowing with certainty what lay behind the door, but Carter was confident that it was the Burial Chamber.

Opposite: The mud plaster that covered the stones with which the doorway had been closed was almost completely covered with impressions of seals. The basket obscures the robber's hole.

Above: The doorway almost completely open and showing the side of a wooden gilded shrine behind it.

At last, Friday 16 February 1923 was set as the date for unblocking the doorway. Carter, Gardiner and Breasted spent the preceding days studying the seal impressions on the plaster of the doorway and were still hard at work in the morning. The two statues were encased in a wooden framework for protection and a wooden platform was built close to the doorway. Chairs were arranged for the guests who were invited to witness the operation – once again, Carter's talent for showmanship was unmistakable.

The proceedings started with short speeches by Carter and Lord Carnarvon at about 2.15pm. Some 20 excavators and guests were present, as well as a number of Egyptian workmen. Carter and Mace, stood on the wooden platform and began to take down the stones of the blocking. Carter loosened each with a hammer, chisel and crowbar, while Mace lifted it. He then carefully lowered it down to Callender who in turn handed it to the first of the Egyptian workmen who formed a human chain along which the stones travelled out of the tomb.

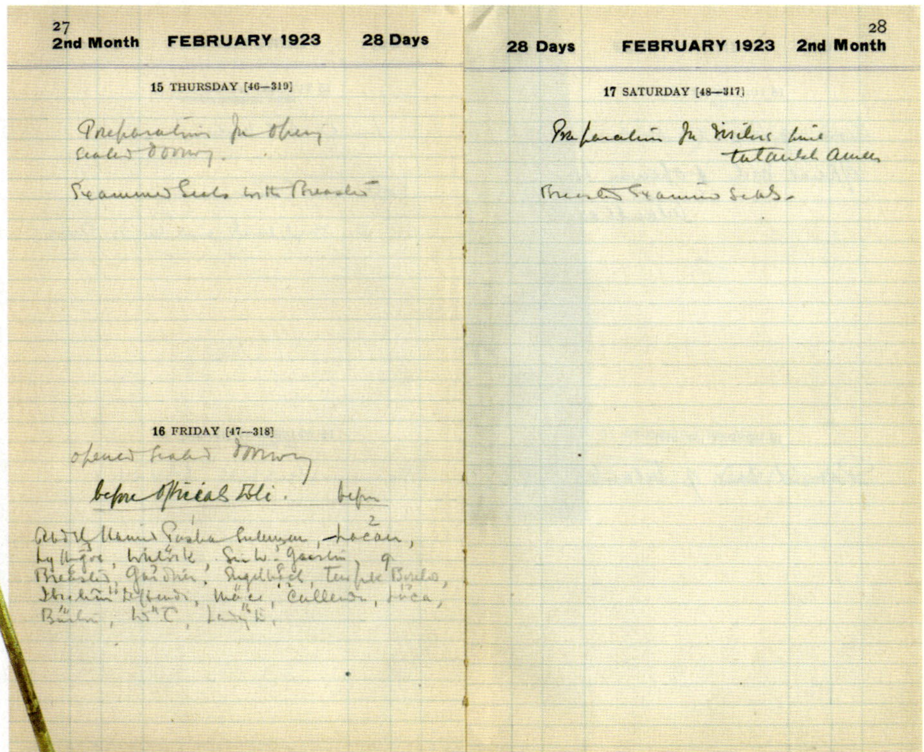
27
2nd Month FEBRUARY 1923 28 Days

15 THURSDAY [46—319]

Preparation for opening sealed doorway.

Examined Seals with Breasted

16 FRIDAY [47—318]

Opened sealed doorway

before officials.

28 Days FEBRUARY 1923 2nd Month
28

17 SATURDAY [48—317]

Breasted Examined Seals.

AN EARLY ENTRY

It is possible that Carter, Lord Carnarvon and Lady Evelyn used a robbers' hole in the blocking of the sealed doorway and "unofficially" visited the Burial Chamber shortly after the opening of the Antechamber on 26 November 1922. This might explain why Carter was so sure that the room behind the doorway was the Burial Chamber.

When the breach was sufficiently large, Carter peered inside with the help of an electric torch. What confronted the excavators appeared to be a solid gold wall decorated with protective symbols and inlaid in blue faience. It was surmised that this was a side of a large wooden gilded shrine, which probably concealed a coffin of Tutankhamun, and the room was the Burial Chamber. Had Carter known all along?

After more of the door blocking had been removed, Carter crawled inside and established that there was just enough room between the front of the shrine and the wall on the right. The guests were then invited, two at a time, to examine the Burial Chamber – access was not easy as the floor is lower than that of the Antechamber. The shrine fitted the room very tightly, its open door was on the visitors' left. Beguilingly beautiful objects could be glimpsed between it and yet another shrine inside.

Another fascinating sight confronted the visitors when they looked to their right. There was another room, later known as the Treasury. Unlike the other doors in the tomb, it was not closed and through it they could see a variety of objects in what appeared to be organised disarray: boxes and shrines, some with their doors open and revealing statuettes inside; models of boats; vessels; parts of chariots; sticks; and staves of bows. The item that attracted most attention, however, was a large shrine with statuettes of four goddesses against the sides, as if forming a protective circle around it. This, as the excavators thought, eventually proved to contain the King's embalmed viscera.

Although everybody's curiosity was severely strained, the Burial Chamber had to wait for the next excavation season. There was still much recording of the objects that had already been removed to the expedition's "laboratory" (the tomb of Sety II) to be done.

THE STATUES OF TUTANKHAMUN

Inscriptions on the two large black and gold statues identify them as showing King Tutankhamun. The term "guardian statues", which is often applied to them, is, however, modern. Their position outside the door into the Burial Chamber is reminiscent of statues flanking gates of temples. They are 172 and 172.3 cm (67.8 and 67.9 in) high – about the same size as the King himself. They are made of wood covered with gesso and black resin (for the flesh parts) or cloth glued to the wood, gesso and gold leaf.

Opposite, left: One of the two "guardian statues" flanking the doorway to the Burial Chamber. The King is wearing the nemes (royal headcloth) with a protective cobra.

Opposite, right: Pages from Howard Carter's pocket diary for 1923 in which he recorded the events surrounding the opening of the door to the Burial Chamber.

Right: The objects found between the outermost and second shrines included alabaster perfume vases in fancifully elaborate forms. A linen pall with gold rosettes sewn onto it, which was placed over the second shrine can be seen between them.

THE BURIAL CHAMBER

The Burial Chamber was opened on 16 February 1923, and the recording and removal of its contents took Carter and his team the next three years. It is the only room in which the walls were smoothed, plastered and decorated with painted scenes.

Above: The massive first (exterior) shrine, made of wood covered with gesso and sheet gold and inlaid with blue faience.
Opposite: Carter (centre), Callender (right) and two Egyptian workmen busy with the first (exterior) shrine.

It has been suggested that Tutankhamun had been entombed before the paint had a chance to dry

There are three genres of representation: (1) scenes characteristic of the Amarna period (for example, a depiction of the funeral); (2) scenes belonging to the earlier tradition showing the King in the company of the gods; (3) a vignette (illustration) from Amduat ("That which is in the Underworld"), one of the "books of the afterlife" (texts that accompanied the individual into the Underworld and facilitated his nightly journey through it). The logical progression of the scenes on the walls of the Burial Chamber is east, north, south, west.

Tutankhamun's funeral, during which a sledge with a shrine containing the King's mummy is dragged to the tomb by palace official (including two viziers), is depicted on the east wall. There are three other scenes on the north wall. From the right: Tutankhamun's successor, King Aye, holds an adze and performs an "opening the mouth" ceremony (its aim was to restore the body's sensory perception) on Tutankhamun, who is shown as the god Osiris (the ruler of the Underworld); the sky goddess Nut welcomes Tutankhamun to the celestial realm traditionally inhabited by dead kings; Tutankhamun, followed by his ka ("life energy" or similar), embraces the god Osiris.

The south wall includes the inner side of the blocked doorway, which was partly destroyed during the opening of the Burial Chamber. On this, the deceased King is led by the jackal-headed necropolis god Anubis to the goddess Hathor, the "chieftainess of the west" (the west was the traditional realm of

"We felt that we were in the presence of the dead King and must do him reverence, and in imagination could see the doors of the successive shrines open one after the other till the innermost disclosed the King himself."

H Carter and A C Mace, The Tomb of Tut-Ankh-Amen, Volume I

Opposite: Carter, Callender, Mace and two Egyptian workmen opening the door of the first (exterior) shrine. A superb picture, but one that may have been set up after the actual event.

Above, left: Eleven wooden oars were found in the space between the outer shrine and the north wall of the Burial Chamber.

Above, right: The open doors of the inner shrines protecting the sarcophagus and coffins.

Right: This life-sized, wooden goose, about 40.4 cm (15.9 in) tall, was found against the east wall of the Burial Chamber. The goose was covered with linen and coated in black resin.

the dead and Hathor appears here as a necropolis goddess). The goddess Isis, standing behind Anubis, welcomes the King. The scene contains a visual pun because the zig-zag "objects" held by the goddess are hieroglyphs reading eni, "to me!". There are three Underworld deities behind Isis. Finally, the west wall has a "vignette" from Amduat that illustrates a stage in the King's journey through the Underworld with five deities, a solar barque and 12 baboons.

Almost all the space in the Burial Chamber was taken up by arrangements that protected the King's mummified body. The royal mummy was lying on its back in the east-west direction, with its head towards the west. It was placed in three coffins contained in a quartzite sarcophagus. The whole assembly was covered by a series of three inner shrines (counting from the outside, the second to fourth), a frame for a decorative pall and a massive outer shrine (the first).

Various objects were deposited in the narrow space between the shrines and the walls of the Burial Chamber, most noticeably a number of oars that were placed next to the north wall in reference to a religious spell in one of the "books of the afterlife" (these books were often inscribed on tomb walls, but here the objects usually shown in them were real). Other items often found in coffins, such as bows and fans, were also placed between the shrines.

Above: Painted scenes on the north wall of the Burial Chamber.
Opposite, left: King Aye performing an "opening the mouth" ceremony on the mummy of Tutankhamun.
Opposite, right: Tutankhamun is welcomed by the sky goddess Nut.

THE FIGURES REPRESENTED IN THE WALL PAINTINGS

KING AYE

Aye was Tutankhamun's successor, of non-royal blood, who came to the throne as a middle-aged man. His reign lasted for only four years and he was buried in Tomb KV 23, in the west branch of the Valley of the Kings.

THE GOD OSIRIS

Osiris was the ruler of the Underworld and was usually shown as a mummy holding a sceptre and a flagellum (flail). His presence in the tomb indicates that the return to the old religious values was well advanced under Tutankhamun.

THE GODDESS NUT

Nut was a sky goddess, usually represented as a woman or a cow. She was included in the tomb's decoration because of the early beliefs in the celestial destiny of the deceased king.

THE GODDESS HATHOR

Hathor was one of the most popular goddess deities worshipped at various places in Egypt, often in the form of a cow. She was one of the deities of the Theban necropolis.

THE GOD ANUBIS

Anubis, usually shown jackal-headed or as a jackal, was the god of the necropolis par excellence.

THE SARCOPHAGUS AND COFFINS

OCTOBER – DECEMBER 1925

Tutankhamun's body was protected by a nest of three coffins, one inside another, like a set of Russian dolls. They were placed on a wooden, gilded bier contained in a quartzite sarcophagus. In Egyptian thinking, the figure three conveyed multiplicity and so Tutankhamun's body was protected by "many" coffins. The coffins are anthropoid (human-shaped), a form that was introduced at the beginning of the 2nd millennium bc. The sarcophagus, with a concave cornice at the top, is traditionally royal and had already been used by pharaohs in the mid-3rd millennium BC.

The lid of the sarcophagus was lifted on 12 February 1924, and the opening of the coffins took place between October and December 1925.

TUESDAY, 13 OCTOBER

Pulleys were used to lift the lid of the first (outermost) coffin. This revealed a second (middle) coffin, which was covered by a linen shroud.

SATURDAY, 17 OCTOBER

The wreath, garlands and shroud were removed from the lid of the second coffin. The first coffin and its contents (the second and third coffins with the mummy) were lifted to just above the level of the sarcophagus.

THURSDAY, 22 OCTOBER

Metal eyelets were screwed into the lower part of the first coffin so that it could be manoeuvred by ropes and pulleys.

Opposite: The goddess Nephthys is shown in a gesture of protection at one corner of the sarcophagus.

Above: The upper part of the lid of the first (outermost) coffin.

SCALE 1/10
172
173
174
175
176
177
178
179
180
181
182
183
184
185
186
187
188
189
190
191
192
193
194
195
196
197
198
199
201
202
203
204
205
206
207
208
210
211
212
214
215
216
217
218
222
223
224
225-230
234
235
237
238
239
240
241
242
243
244
245
246
247
248
249
250
251
252, 253.
(254-6)
253A
257
258
259
260

FRIDAY, 23 OCTOBER
The first coffin was lowered back into the sarcophagus. The second coffin was placed on a wooden tray over the sarcophagus and its removed, revealing the third (innermost) coffin, covered by a shroud of reddish colour with a floral collar. The second and third coffins were found to be fixed together by the solidified material that had been poured over them during the funeral.

SUNDAY, 25 OCTOBER
The second coffin, containing the third coffin (and the mummy), was moved from the Burial Chamber into the Antechamber, where there was more space for work.

WEDNESDAY, 28 OCTOBER
The lid of the third coffin was removed. This revealed the wrapped mummy of Tutankhamun with its now famous gold mask.

WEDNESDAY, 4 NOVEMBER
The lower part of the first coffin was raised from the sarcophagus by pulleys and moved into the Antechamber.

Opposite: Howard Carter's plan of the Burial Chamber showing how the coffins were arranged inside the sarcophagus and shrines.
Above: Manoeuvring the second coffin (with the third coffin and the mummy still inside) out of the lower half of the first (outermost) coffin.

THE COFFINS

THE FIRST (OUTERMOST) COFFIN

Anthropoid (human-shaped), made of wood which was covered with gesso and gold foil. A wreath consisting of olive leaves and perhaps blue cornflowers was placed over the insignia on the forehead of the sarcophagus. The figures of the goddesses Isis and Nephthys are represented on the coffin as though enfolding the deceased King in their wings. The feet of the coffin had been partly cut off in antiquity because they were too high to fit under the lid of the main sarcophagus.

THE SECOND (MIDDLE) COFFIN

Anthropoid, made of wood covered with gesso and gold foil. It was covered with a linen shroud and a wreath and flower garlands were placed on it. The two protective goddesses, Nekhbet and Wadjet, are represented as vulture- and serpent-headed birds just below the King's crossed arms.

THE THIRD (INNERMOST) COFFIN

Anthropoid, made of solid gold, 2.5–3 mm (approx. 0.1 in) thick, weighing 110.4 kg (244 lb). The goddesses Nekhbet and Wadjet as vulture- and serpent-headed birds with outstretched wings are shown over the King's abdomen and his crossed forearms. The goddesses Isis and Nephthys are represented as women with outstretched wings over the King's legs.

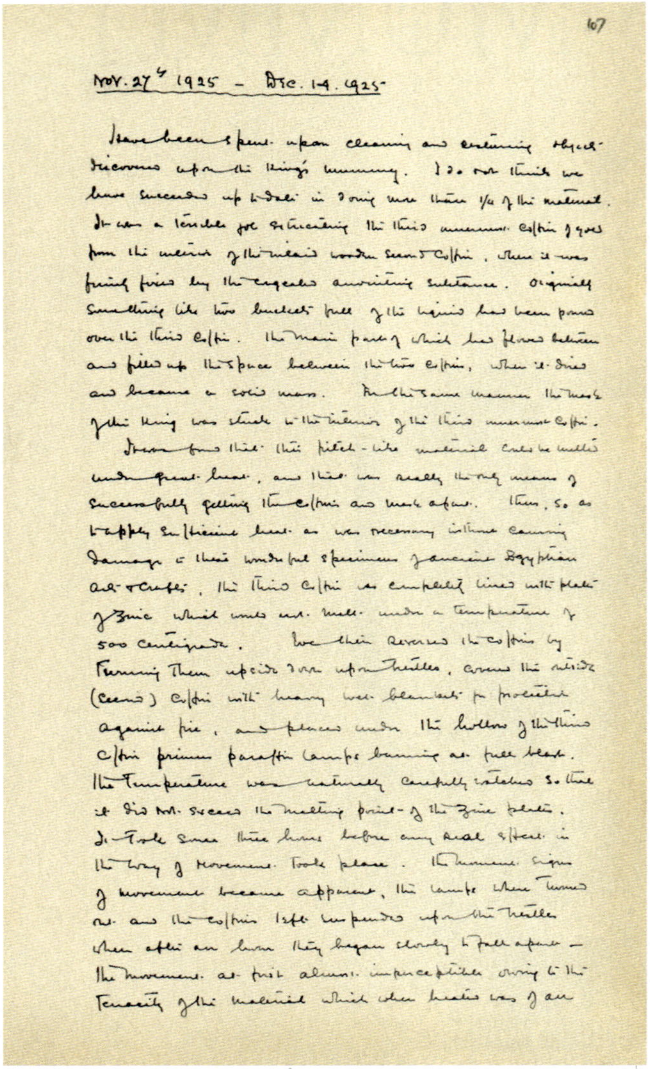

107

Nov. 27th 1925 – Dec. 14. 1925.

Have been spent upon cleaning and restoring objects discovered upon the King's mummy. I do not think we have succeeded up to date in doing more than 1/4 of the material. It was a terrible job extricating the third innermost coffin of gold from the interior of the weird wooden second coffin, where it was firmly fixed by the congealed anointing substance. Originally something like two buckets full of the liquid had been poured over the third coffin. The main part of which had flowed between and filled up the space between the two coffins, where it dried and became a solid mass. In the same manner the mask of the King was stuck to the interior of the third innermost coffin.

I soon found that this pitch-like material could be melted under great heat, and that was really the only means of successfully getting the coffins and mask apart. Thus, so as to apply sufficient heat as was necessary without causing damage to these wonderful specimens of ancient Egyptian Art & Crafts, the third coffin was completely lined with plates of zinc which would not melt under a temperature of 500 centigrade. We then reversed the coffins by turning them upside down upon trestles, covered the outside (second) coffin with heavy wet blankets for protection against fire, and placed under the hollow of the third coffin primus paraffin lamps burning at full blast. The temperature was naturally carefully watched so that it did not exceed the melting point of the zinc plates. It took some three hours before any real effect in the way of movement took place. The moment signs of movement became apparent, the lamps where turned out and the coffins left suspended upon the trestles when after an hour they began slowly to fall apart — the movement at first almost imperceptible owing to the tenacity of the material which when heated was of an

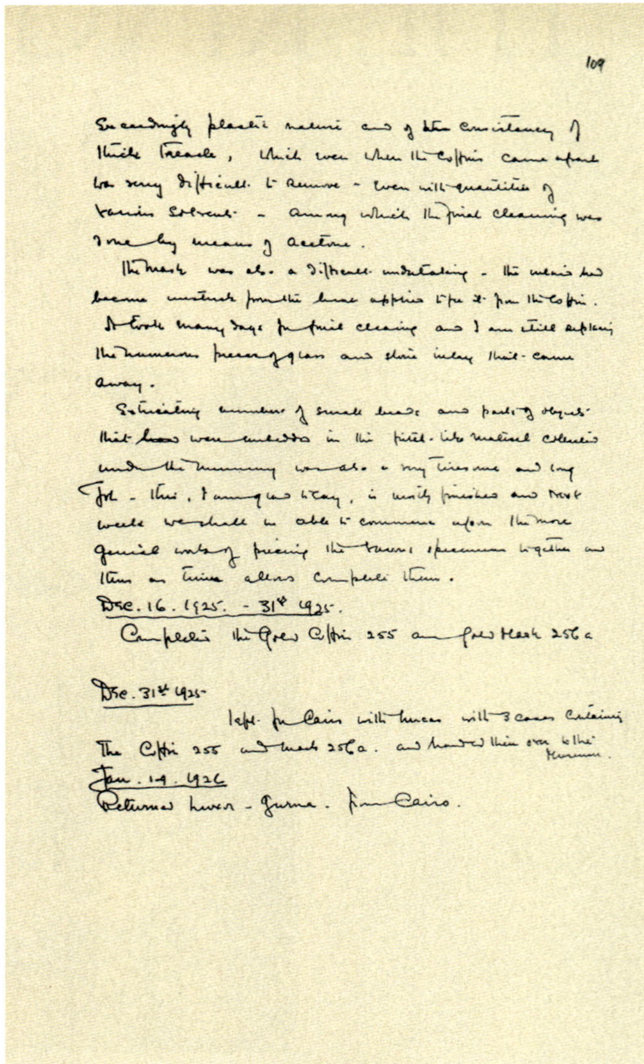

109

exceedingly plastic nature and of the consistency of thick treacle, which even when the coffins came apart was very difficult to remove – even with quantities of various solvents – among which the final cleaning was done by means of acetone.

The mask was also a difficult undertaking – the resin had become unstuck from the heat applied to free it from the coffin. It took many days for final cleaning and I am still replacing the numerous pieces of glass and stone inlay that came away.

Extricating numbers of small beads and parts of objects that have been embedded in the pitch-like material collected under the mummy was also a very tiresome and long job – this, I am glad to say, is nearly finished and next week we shall be able to commence upon the more genial work of piecing the various specimens together and then as time allows complete them.

Dec. 16. 1925. – 31st 1925.

Completing the Gold Coffin 255 and Gold Mask 256a

Dec. 31st 1925.

Left for Cairo with Lucas with 3 cases containing The Coffin 255 and Mask 256a. and handed them over to the Museum.

Jan. 14. 1926

Returned Luxor – Qurna. from Cairo.

THURSDAY, 5 NOVEMBER
The bier on which the coffins rested was lifted out from the sarcophagus.

WEDNESDAY, 11 NOVEMBER – THURSDAY, 19 NOVEMBER
The unwrapping and examination of Tutankhamun's mummy, which had been removed to the "laboratory" in tomb KV 15. The gold mask remained stuck to the interior of the third coffin.

FRIDAY, 27 NOVEMBER – MONDAY, 14 DECEMBER
The second and third coffins, glued together by the solidified mass of libations, were separated. This was achieved by lining the third (inner), coffin with zinc plates, turning the coffins upside down, covering the outside of the second coffin with heavy blankets to protect it against fire, and placing paraffin lamps under the third coffin in order to melt the solidified material. It took three hours before the coffins separated. The gold mask was freed from the third coffin during the same operation.

Opposite: Carter and an Egyptian assistant cleaning the lid of the third coffin, which is still inside the second coffin and is made of solid gold.

Above: Pages from Howard Carter's excavation journal for 27 November 1925–14 February 1926, in which he describes dismantling the shrines and exposing the sarcophagus.

THE KING'S MUMMY

11—19 NOVEMBER 1925

Tutankhamun's mummy was unwrapped and examined in November 1925, some three years after the discovery of the tomb and more than two and a half years after the opening of the Burial Chamber. The body was lying on its back, with the arms folded on the chest, entirely wrapped up in bandages and covered with a linen sheet. It was in a poor state of preservation.

Above: Gold pectoral (breast ornament) in the form of a human-headed bird, sewn onto the outer wrapping of the mummy.

Opposite: Tutankhamun's mummy with a gold mask and hands attached to the outer wrappings.

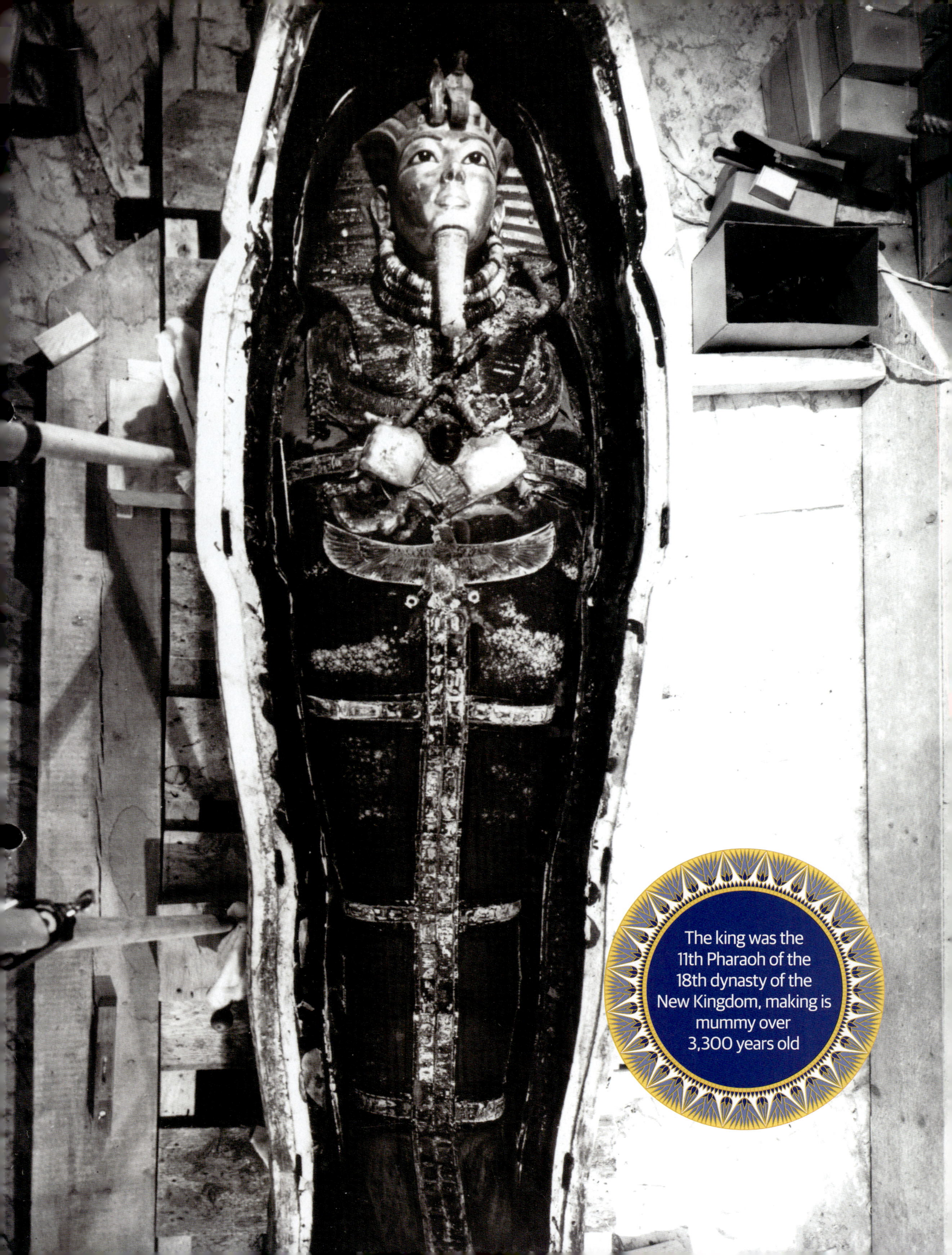

The king was the 11th Pharaoh of the 18th dynasty of the New Kingdom, making is mummy over 3,300 years old

The examination was made more difficult by the fact that the mummy was firmly stuck to the bottom of the innermost coffin by a pitch-like substance, the solidified libations which had been poured over it during the funeral. The same was true of the gold mask covering the mummy's head and shoulders (this was not freed until after the examination of the mummy) and of the middle and innermost coffins themselves.

The lower halves of the second (middle) and third (innermost) coffins and their contents were removed to the "laboratory" and the examination was carried out with the mummy still lying inside the innermost coffin.

It was performed by two physicians, Douglas E Derry, Professor of Anatomy of the School of Medicine in Cairo, and Saleh Bey Hamdi, the School's former Director, in the presence of a number of guests who included Pierre Lacau, the Director General of the Antiquities Service, and Tewfik Boulos, the Chief Inspector for Upper Egypt. It was a long-drawn-out affair and Carter complained in his journal about the guests' impatience and dislike of the delays required for the recording and taking of photographs.

The living height of the King was estimated to have been 167.6 cm (66 in) but the examination did not reveal the cause of the Pharaoh's death. Historically, its most important result was the belief that Tutankhamun was about 18 years old at the time of his death (the most recent examination adjusted this to 19 years).

WEDNESDAY, 11 NOVEMBER 1925

The procedures began with applying melted paraffin to the mummy's very fragile outer wrappings in order to solidify them before they were removed. Soon it became apparent that the condition of the bandages closer to the body was even worse and this made it impossible to establish a pattern in which the bandages had been applied (later, Carter counted altogether 16 layers of bandages). An oval plaque was found inserted in the wrappings over the mummy's left flank (this was almost always the location of the incision through which the inner organs were removed). Various amulets, jewellery and other objects, including a dagger, mostly made of gold, were found as the unwrapping proceeded. (A week later, when the examination was completed, Carter wrote that there were 97 groups of items found in the wrappings.)

THURSDAY, 12 NOVEMBER 1925

The mummy wrappings and the objects placed among them and on the body, including another dagger, were completely removed from the lower half of the body, as well as the right arm and hand, which wore bracelets, rings and finger stalls (to prevent the loss of nails). The exposed skin was greyish white and displayed many cracks.

FRIDAY, 13 NOVEMBER 1925

The exposed fragile parts of the body were treated with hot paraffin. Wrappings were removed from the left arm, revealing rings and bracelets.

SATURDAY, 14 NOVEMBER 1925

All the limbs and the body as far as the shoulders were now uncovered. Small and almost completely destroyed fragments of papyri inscribed with cursive hieroglyphs were found but

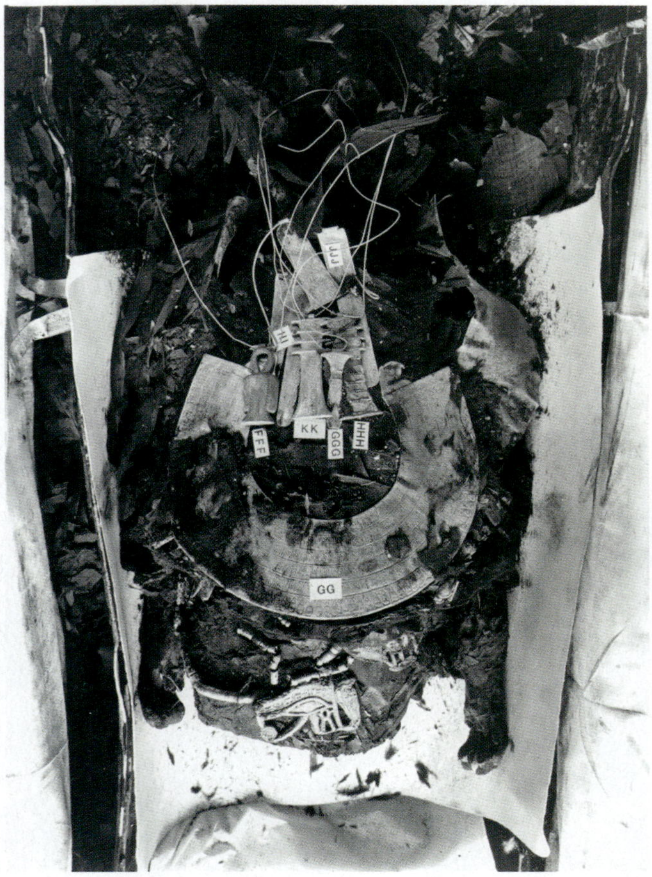

Above: Various amulets, a gold hawk collar over the mummy's pectoral area and a blue faience "eye of the god Horus" over the abdomen.

Opposite: Tutankhamun's head after it was laboriously detached from the bottom of the innermost coffin.

Overleaf: Howard Carter's drawings recording the successive stages of unwrapping the mummy and the arrangement of objects on the body.

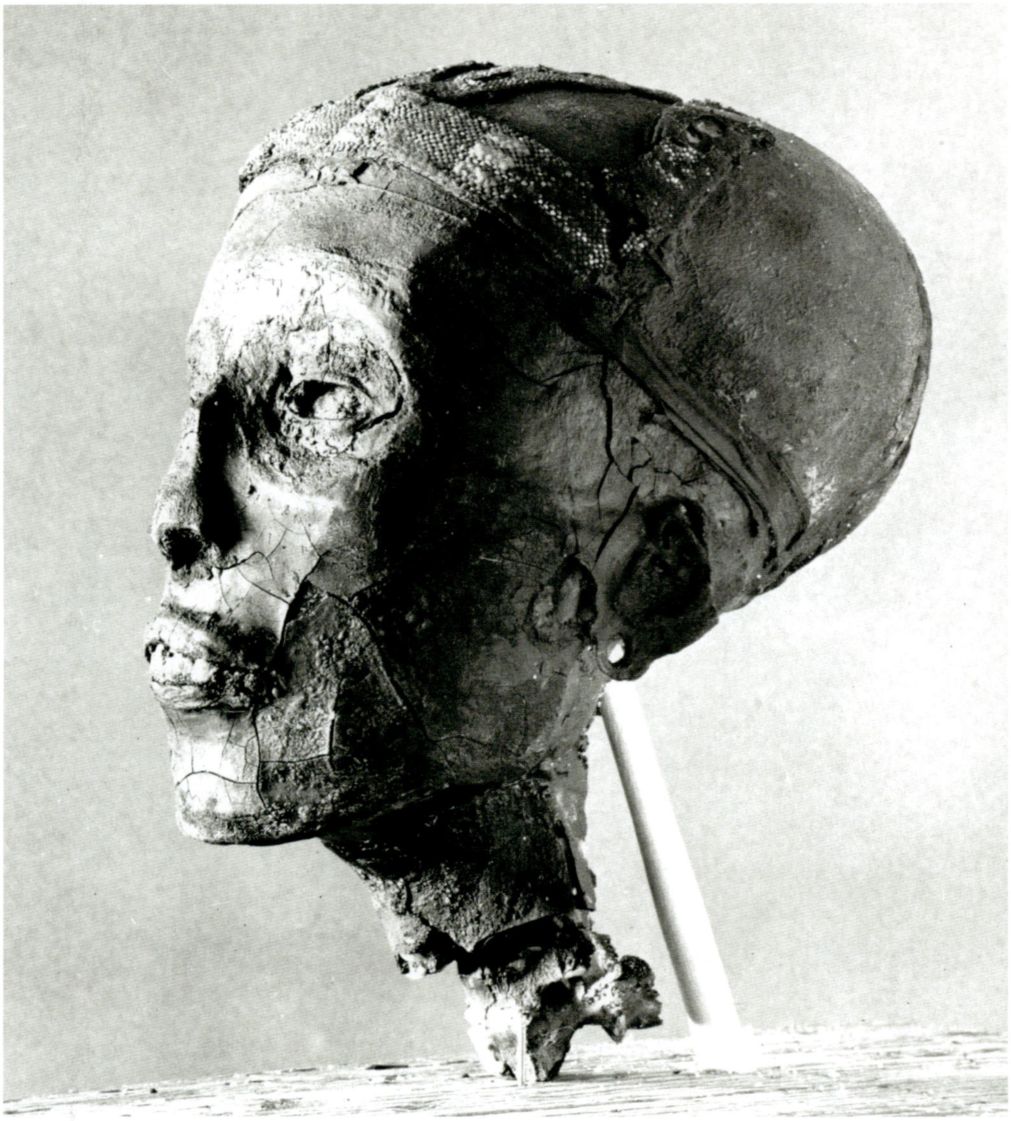

MUMMIFICATION

The Egyptians believed that preservation of the body was one of the preconditions for successful rebirth and continued life after death. The three main stages of the mummification process were the removal of the internal organs (these were usually kept separately from the body), the desiccation of the body's tissues by packing it with and burying it in natron (a naturally occurring dehydrating agent) and an elaborate wrapping of the body in a series of linen bandages. The term "mummy" derives from Arabic mumiya, "bitumen", from the blackened appearance of many mummies. No secret techniques or substances were employed; various fragrant substances and others which were intended to purify the body were applied but they played hardly any part in the actual preservation of the body.

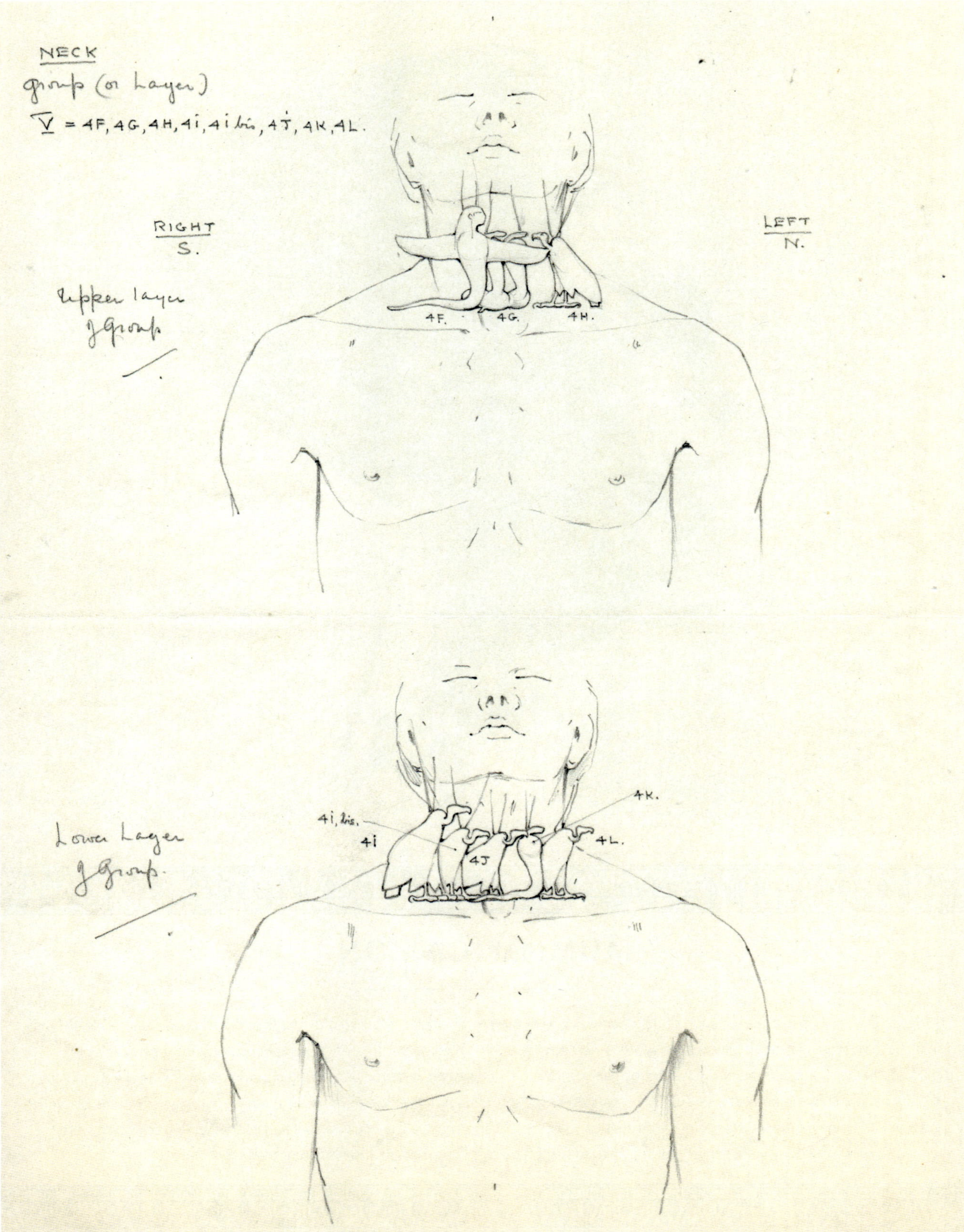
NECK
Group (or Layer)
V = 4F, 4G, 4H, 4i, 4i bis, 4J, 4K, 4L.
RIGHT
S.
LEFT
N.
Upper layer of Group
4F.
4G.
4H.
Lower Layer of Group
4i, bis.
4i
4J
4K.
4L.

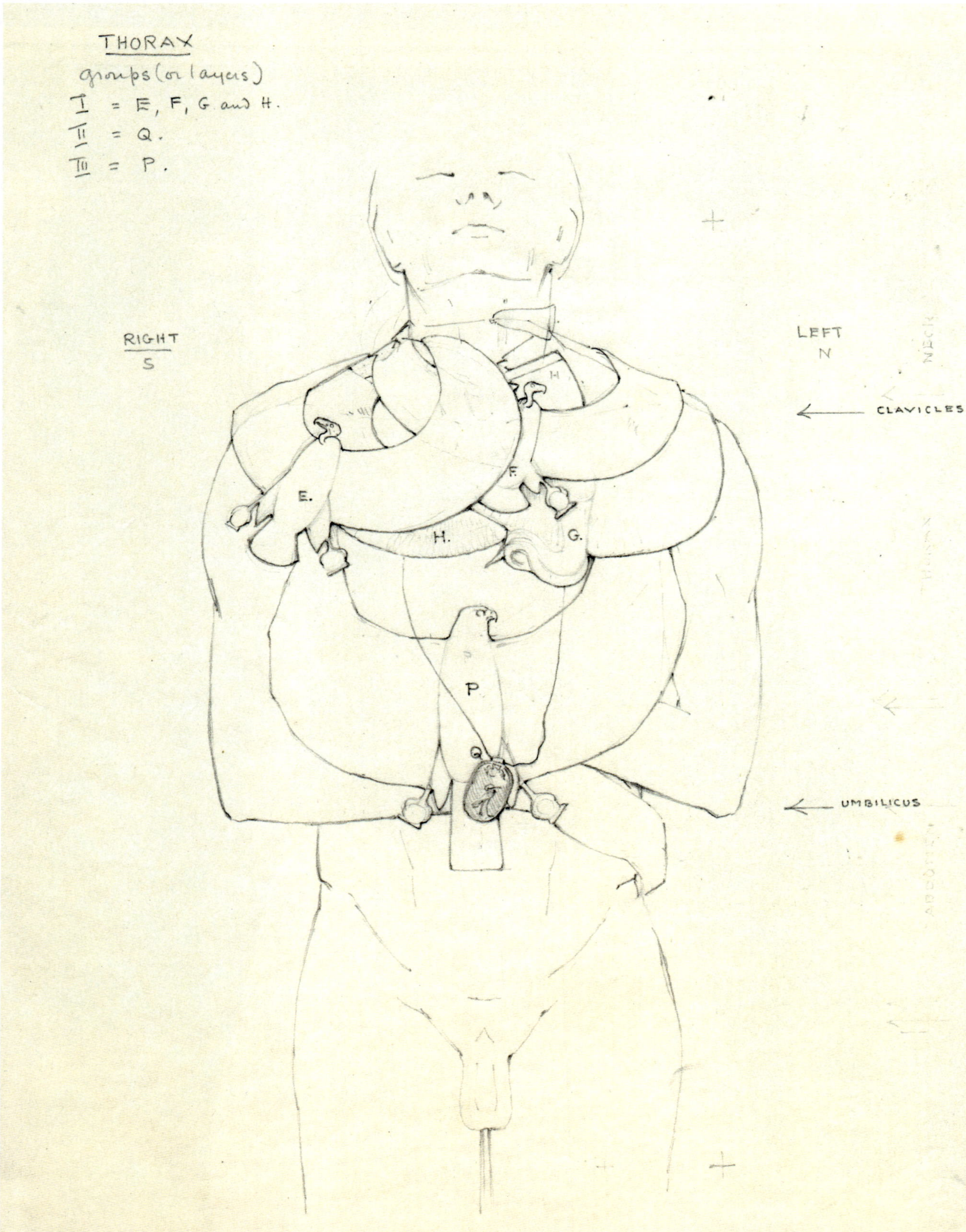
THORAX
groups (or layers)
I = E, F, G and H.
II = Q.
III = P.
RIGHT
S
LEFT
N
NECK
CLAVICLES
UMBILICUS
E.
F.
H.
G.
P
Q

these were probably connected with amulets and did not contain any substantial texts (otherwise, no papyri were found in the tomb).

SUNDAY, 15 NOVEMBER 1925
At the end of the day only the head still remained to be examined.

MONDAY, 16 NOVEMBER 1925
The head was firmly stuck to the bottom of the innermost coffin and had to be separated with hot knives. Carter wrote that "the face has beautiful and well formed features".

THURSDAY, 19 NOVEMBER 1925
The examination was completed by taking final measurements of the head.

Opposite: Some of the guests that were present at the unwrapping of Tutankhamun's mummy, including Pierre Lacau, the Director General of the Antiquities Service (right).

Above: Gold pectoral showing three scarabs inlaid with lapis lazuli, found suspended from the King's neck.

Right: Tutankhamun's reconstructed appearance based on CT scans made in 2005.

THE LATER EXAMINATIONS OF THE MUMMY

The Egyptians believed that preservation of the body was one of the preconditions for successful rebirth and continued life after death. The three main stages of the mummification process were the removal of the internal organs (these were usually kept separately from the body), the desiccation of the body's tissues by packing it with and burying it in natron (a naturally occurring dehydrating agent) and an elaborate wrapping of the body in a series of linen bandages. The term "mummy" derives from Arabic mumiya, "bitumen", from the blackened appearance of many mummies. No secret techniques or substances were employed; various fragrant substances and others which were intended to purify the body were applied but they played hardly any part in the actual preservation of the body.

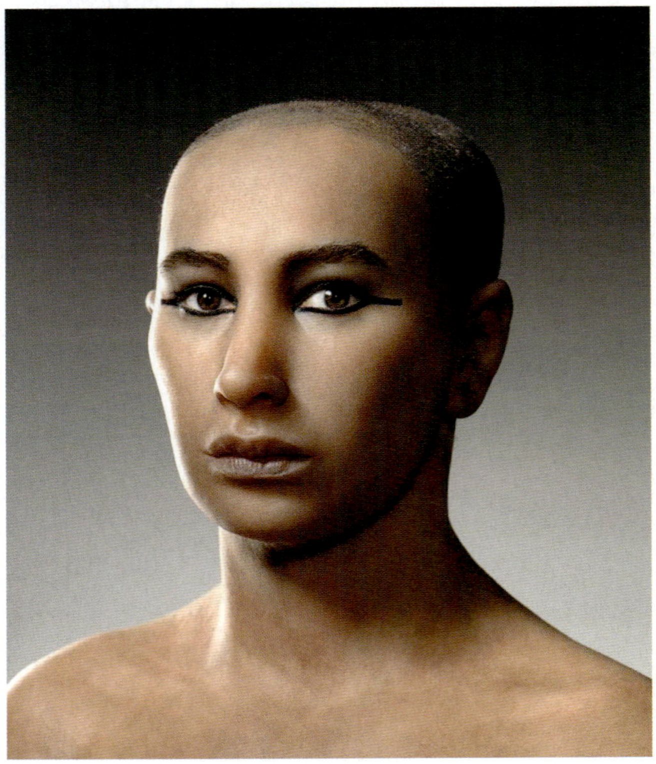

THE TREASURY

OCTOBER 1926 – OCTOBER 1927

The room to the east of the Burial Chamber was called "The Treasury" by Carter, and although this is a somewhat misleading term, it will be retained here. The excavators were able to glimpse its contents when they entered the Burial Chamber on 16 February 1923. However, they did not start examining and recording the objects and removing them to the "laboratory" and then to the Cairo Museum until more than three years later.

Opposite: A black chest in the form of a shrine, which contained five large, wooden statues of Tutankhamun

Above: A wooden model of a sailing boat that measures 93.4 cm (36.8 in).

"Compared with the Antechamber and the Annexe, the room was found relatively undisturbed. It was dominated by the shrine with carrying poles and a figure of the necropolis god Anubis in the form of a jackal. This was, no doubt, used during Tutankhamun's funeral and was laid down in the doorway facing towards the shrines with coffins. At the innermost end of the room was a chest containing a box with the King's viscera, which would have been removed during mummification.

The majority of items deposited in this room were contained in wooden, box-like shrines. There were statuettes of deities (mostly those connected with the Underworld rather than the main state gods) and shabtis (figures that served as "substitutes" when the King was asked to perform manual tasks in the Underworld). Larger pieces included sculptures showing Tutankhamun harpooning, perhaps a hippopotamus, from a reed canoe (one of the oldest funerary motifs) and his image being carried on the back of a leopard. There were also model boats for the King's celestial or Underworld journeys.

A wooden box in the north-eastern corner of the room contained coffins with the foetuses of two still-born children. The Treasury also contained two dismantled chariots.

Above and opposite bottom right: The Treasury seen from the doorway connecting it with the Burial Chamber.

Opposite, top left: One of the two prematurely born, mummified children. Each was enclosed in a nest of two gilded anthropoid coffins.

Opposite, below left: View from the Burial Chamber into the Treasury, with the portable Anubis shrine still partly obstructing the doorway.

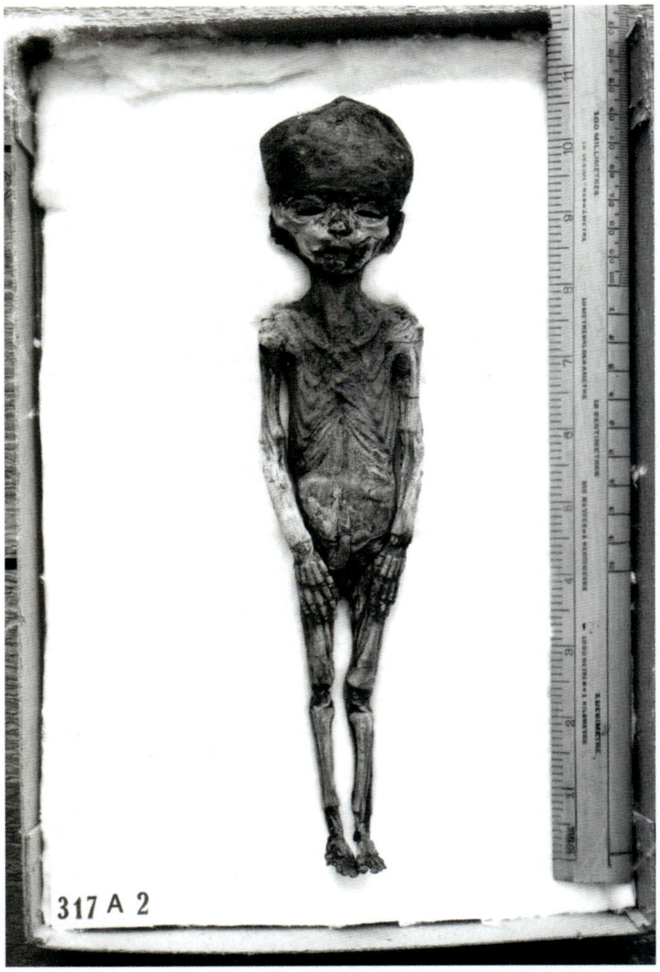

TUTANKHAMUN'S CHILDREN

Burials of small children are rarely found in Egyptian tombs. There is little doubt that the two mummified foetuses found in two pairs of coffins were Tutankhamun's children, almost certainly by Ankhesenamun. Both were girls and the gestation periods are estimated to have been about five and seven months.

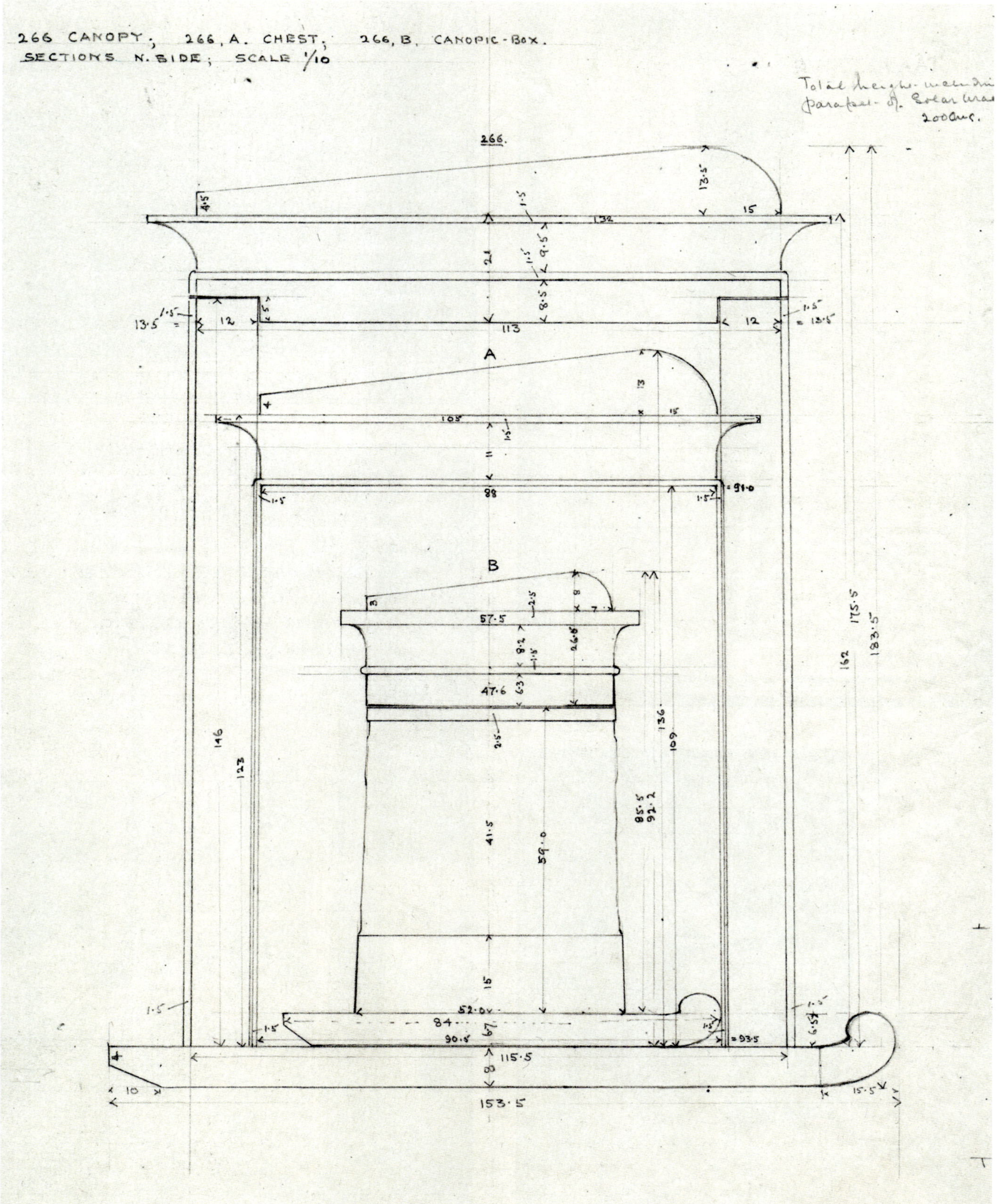
266 CANOPY; 266, A. CHEST; 266, B. CANOPIC-BOX.
SECTIONS N. SIDE; SCALE 1/10
266.
A
B
153·5
115·5

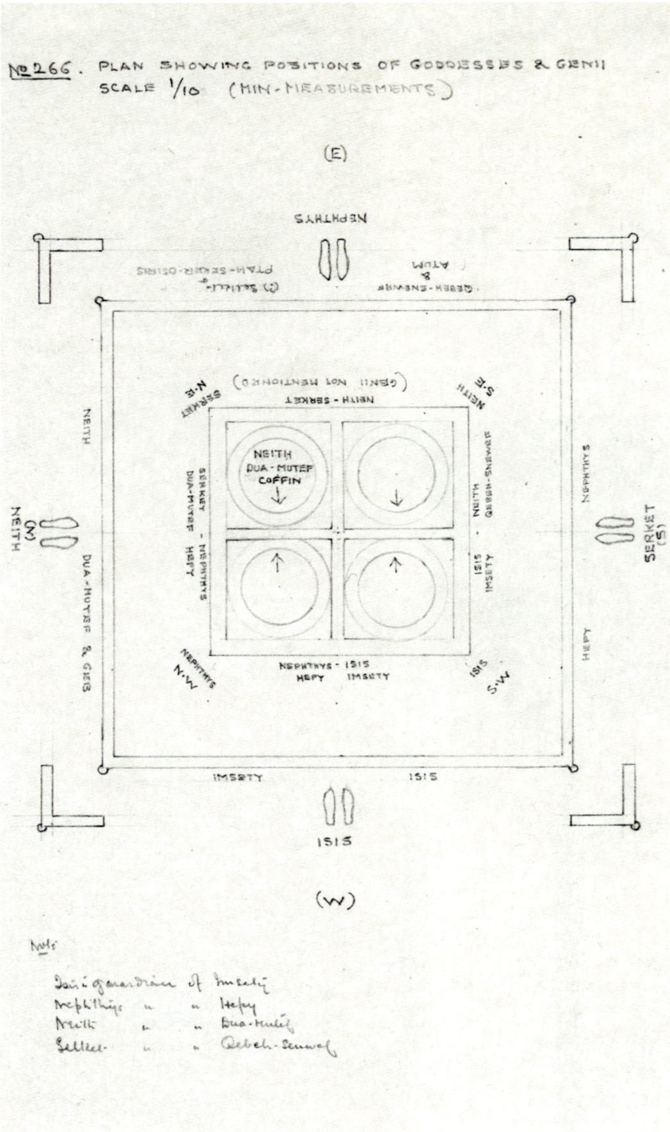

TUTANKHAMUN'S CANOPIC EQUIPMENT

The Egyptians realised early that the internal organs presented the greatest obstacle to the successful preservation of the human body. In recognition of this they removed them – that is, the liver, lungs, stomach and intestines – during mummification, usually by an incision in the left flank. The organs were treated by natron (a drying agent), placed in special containers, called canopic jars by Egyptologists, and kept close to the mummified body of the deceased person. The method chosen for Tutankhamun was similar, but more elaborate. Packages containing the removed organs were put into four miniature gold coffins. These coffins were then inserted into four cavities in an alabaster box in the shape of a shrine with the figures of four protective goddesses (Isis, Nephthys, Neith and Selket) carved at each corner. The cavities were closed by four human-headed stoppers. The box was covered with a linen cloth and placed inside a wooden chest with another set of protective goddesses, each standing against one of its sides. The goddesses form a protective ring around the chest by their outstretched arms and although they face towards the chest, each turns her head towards the visitor. This chest was then placed under a wooden canopy.

Opposite and above: Howard Carter's drawings of the wooden canopy, chest and alabaster canopic box containing the King's viscera.

Right: The alabaster canopic box that contained the King's internal organs.

THE ANNEXE

NOVEMBER 1927–OCTOBER 1930

The small room that Carter called the Annexe can be regarded as an extension of the Antechamber. The two rooms were connected by a doorway, located at the southern end of the west wall of the Antechamber. The door was originally sealed, but it was broken through by robbers who were also responsible for the chaotic state in which the room was found by the excavators. The Annexe's doorway was the only one that had not been re-sealed and it was the last room in the tomb to be recorded and cleared.

The contents of the Annexe were varied. The room was intended to serve as a store for provisions of food and drink for the afterlife, also items such as oils and ointments and possibly some furniture. The small size of the Annexe meant that some objects, which one would usually expect to find there, ended up in the Antechamber.

The overflow of objects makes it possible to reconstruct, in a tentative way, the order in which various items were placed in the tomb. It is likely that the items to be deposited in Tutankhamun's tomb were all brought at the same time, probably during the funeral, and then re-directed into the individual rooms.

1. The Burial Chamber received the most attention and its arrangement was completed first.

2. The Treasury contained items that were closely associated with the King's mummy and was probably filled next. Access from this room into the Burial Chamber was unobstructed. The doorway between the Antechamber and the Burial Chamber was probably partly closed as quickly as possible, in order to allow enough time for tomb artists to complete the decoration on its inside. This might explain why some items, such as model boats and shabti figures, ended up in the Annexe, although there was still enough space for them in the Treasury. It may

BOWS

The bows were found in the Antechamber, the Burial Chamber and the Annexe. There were some 32 composite bows with laminated staves and 14 self bows, as well as arrows, quivers, bow-cases and archer's wrist-guards. Some items are connected with the old custom of putting bows into the coffin; others may have been used by Tutankhamun in his lifetime.

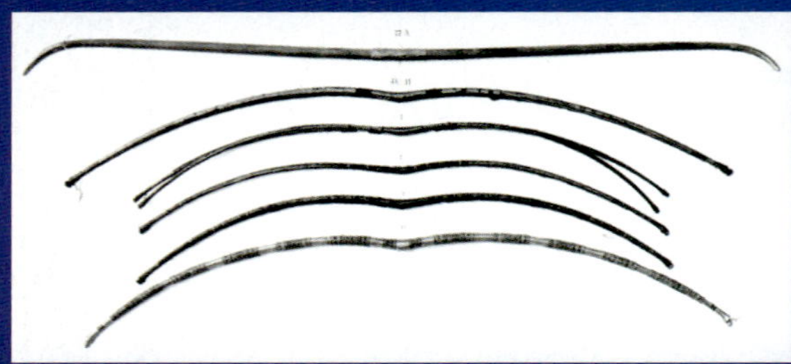

Opposite: A table-shaped box made of ebony and a red-brown wood, partly gilded. The lid is attached by bronze hinges.

Above: A self bow with a simple wooden stave and five composite bows with laminated staves. The latter are recognisable by the typical double-curved shape before stringing.

Left: The door leading from the Antechamber into the Annexe. It was left unsealed after it had been broken through by tomb robbers.

have been an oversight that was too late to put right, perhaps because the doorway to the Antechamber was already partly blocked and it was no longer possible to bring more objects through it.

3. The Annexe was the next room to receive the attention of those that were responsible for putting away the funerary equipment. It was, however, too small for all the items that should have been put into it, and so some food offerings (bread containers) as well as some items of furniture had to be left in the Antechamber.

4. The Antechamber was meant to contain large items that would have been difficult to fit into the other rooms, but finally also had to contain the overflow of objects for which there was not enough room in the Annexe.

MODEL BOATS

In all, 35 wooden model boats were found in Tutankhamun's tomb: 18 in the Treasury and 17 in the Annexe. The majority are sailing boats, but there are also models representing papyrus canoes, ceremonial barges, which were towed by other boats during funerals and official occasions, and barques of the sun god. Their hulls are carved from a solid block of wood. Most of them are about 80 cm (31 in) long, but three of them measure as much as 242 cm (95 in). These models probably represent several different traditions in afterlife beliefs. At least some of them imitate contemporary craft that could be seen on the Nile in Tutankhamun's reign, and were included as substitutes for real boats. Models of papyrus canoes may relate to the traditional tomb scenes of fowling and fishing carried out from such boats. Solar barques were to be used in celestial travels or in journeys that the King was going to undertake in the company of the sun god in the Underworld.

Opposite, far left, from top: The disarray of objects against the west wall, opposite the doorway. They include model boats, baskets and kiosks with shabti figures; Objects piled up against the south wall, with a wooden bow case in the foreground and a bedstead on top of the other items; The north-west corner of the Annexe, with boxes, baskets and pottery jars.

Opposite: One of the model boats imitating contemporary Nile craft, with a central cabin and two large steering oars aft.

Above: A richly inlaid and painted alabaster boat with gazelle heads on the prow and stern, a cabin amidships and two nude girls (one of them originally held an ivory punting pole).

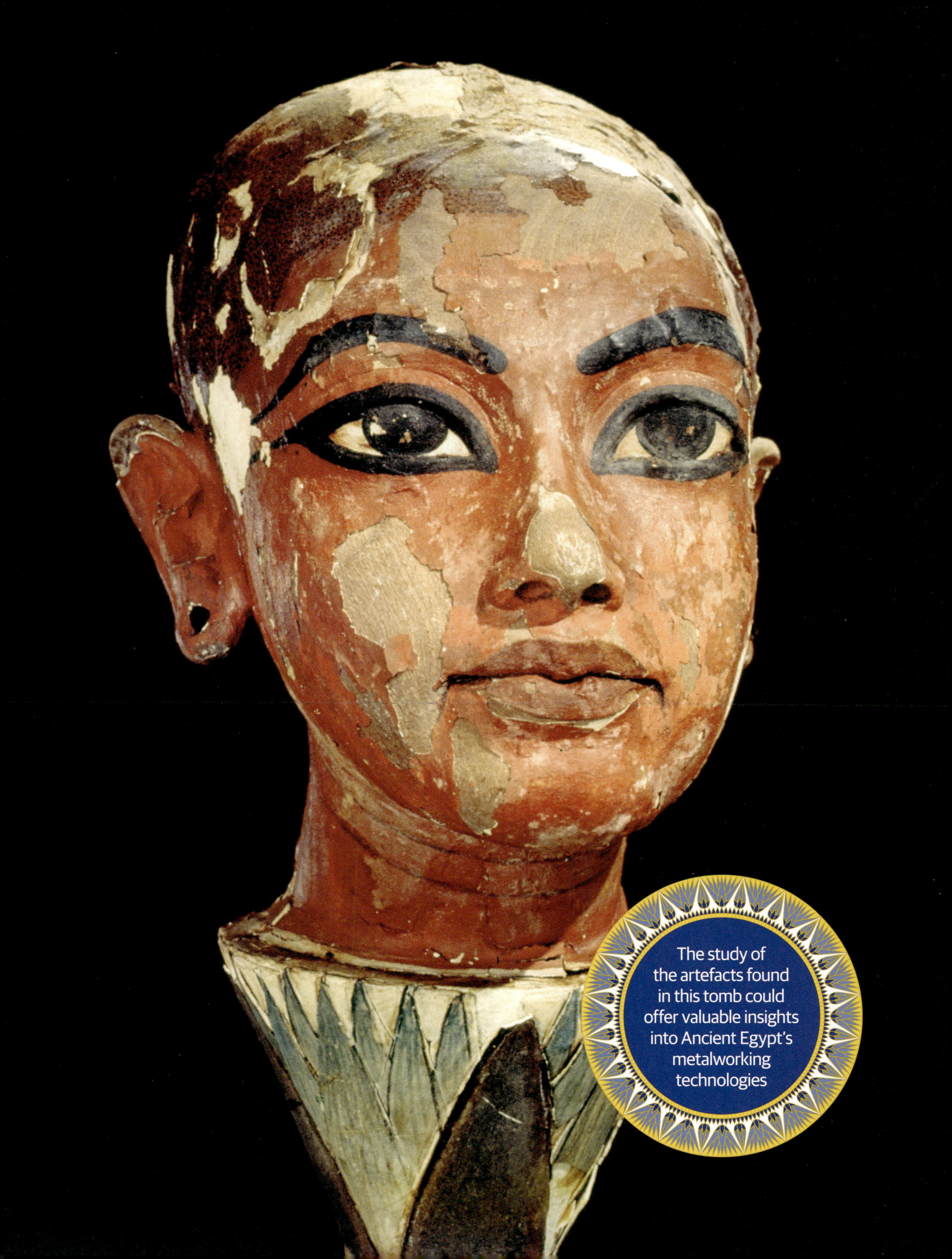

The study of the artefacts found in this tomb could offer valuable insights into Ancient Egypt's metalworking technologies

THE CONTENTS OF THE TOMB

The 5,398 objects that were found in the tomb display a huge range of types and forms. Their distribution in the tomb obscures the fact that they can be divided into several broad categories defined by their purpose. In some cases these overlap or there is some uncertainty about the object's interpretation. Although Tutankhamun's tomb was in many respects unusual, there is little doubt that in this it was almost certainly comparable with other royal tombs. We can only guess at the extent of the riches that were put into tombs of kings such as Amenhotep III or Ramesses II.

Opposite: A wooden painted head on a lotus (a symbol of resurrection). It was found in the filling of the Descending Passage.

Above: Tutankhamun's mummified hand with finger stalls, which were to prevent the loss of nails, and rings.

The reasons for the presence of various objects in Tutankhamun's tomb were:

1. To protect and preserve the King's body (items in the Burial Chamber and the Treasury).

The physical preservation of Tutankhamun's body was essential for his afterlife. The King's body was mummified (treated in order to prevent its decay and wrapped in bandages), provided with a gold mask over the King's head (to protect the most individual part of the body and identify it) and with various other devices (for example, finger and toe stalls to prevent the loss of nails), and placed into a set of three coffins, a sarcophagus and four shrines. The internal organs removed during mummification were put into a canopic box.

2. To safeguard the King's afterlife (objects in all parts of the tomb and also includes the paintings on the walls of the Burial Chamber).

In the course of Egyptian history, the concept of "heaven" to which the Egyptian king departed after his death was altered several times. The beliefs occasionally appear contradictory. At first, the king was thought to have flown to the starry sky to become one of the circumpolar stars. When in the middle of the 3rd millennium BC belief in Osiris gained widespread acceptance, the king was identified with him and his afterlife existence was relegated to a vaguely located Underworld region (Osiris was originally an earth god). From the mid-2nd millennium BC, and especially after the Amarna period, the king was thought to participate in the nightly journey of the sun god through the Underworld in order to re-appear, like the

CHESTS AND BOXES

Wooden chests and boxes were the most common items of furniture after beds, chairs and low tables. They were used for universal storage of all kinds of articles, including clothes that were kept folded up (wardrobes where they could be kept hanging were not known). Chests and boxes were found in all rooms of the tomb except for the Burial Chamber. They contained a variety of objects and so span several of the categories listed above. A painted box on four, square legs with a round lid from the Antechamber is the most striking example. It contained a headrest, sandals, various garments, some jewellery, rolls of linen and pads of cloth. Its sides and lid are decorated with imaginary scenes showing Tutankhamun in his chariot waging war on Nubians and Syrians.

sun in the morning, reborn after death and able to continue his afterlife existence.

3. To maintain the King's royal status in the afterlife (objects in all parts of the tomb).

Despite the complexity of funerary ideas represented in the tomb it was essential that the deceased king would retain his royal status in the afterlife and that he would be able to continue acting as a king.

4. To keep the memory of the King's life on earth alive (mainly objects in the Antechamber and the Annexe).

There is little doubt that many objects found in the tomb were specially made for the King's funeral, probably in haste while the body was being mummified (this usually took at least 70 days), the tomb prepared and the funeral organised. But it is difficult to find religious significance for some items and these were probably brought from the royal palace where they had been used during Tutankhamun's lifetime.

THE COUCHES

The three couches or, perhaps better, elaborate beds found in the Antechamber are almost certainly associated with the King's afterlife in the company of the gods, but exactly how they were intended to function is not clear. It seems that they were specially made for the tomb. Their construction in itself is not unusual. Each of them can be seen as a pair of animals: lionesses as personifications of the goddess Mehytweret, cows of Isis-mehtet, and composite animals with hippopotamus heads of Amemet, the "devourer" of the judgement of the dead. Their bodies form the long sides of the couch and they carry the bed proper between them.

Opposite, top: The hippopotamus head on the Amemet couch.

Opposite: A wooden box, found in the Antechamber, with painted decoration that includes scenes of the King hunting and vanquishing African and Asiatic foes.

Above, left: This white-painted, wooden bed was found in the Antechamber. Linen strips were stretched across the frame to provide support.

Above, right: The cow-headed couch from the Antechamber. The sun disc between the horns was the standard headgear of many goddesses.

Right: This white-painted, wooden bed was found in the Antechamber. Linen strips were stretched across the frame to provide support.

SAFEGUARDING TUTANKHAMUN'S AFTERLIFE

The ideas concerning life after death that we encounter in Tutankhamun's tomb were an amalgam of concepts prevailing at different times (one may think of them as providing for all eventualities). After the King's mummified body in its sarcophagus, coffins and shrines in the Burial Chamber, and his viscera in a canopic chest in the Treasury, the most important features were those which ensured his successful transition from this world into the afterlife and his continued existence there.

Above: One of the two wooden gilded statues of Tutankhamun carried on the back of a black leopard, which were found in the Treasury.
Opposite, above: Some of the baskets and wine jars, containing provisions for the King's afterlife, found in the Annexe.
Opposite, below: Wooden containers for food were piled up under the couches in the Antechamber.

The two- and three-dimensional imagery which is an integral part of the tomb is limited, but it is functional and not merely decorative. It consists of the painted scenes in the Burial Chamber, the "guardian statues" at the entrance to it, and some objects placed inside it (for example, the oars). The purpose of the "magical figures" in the niches was also protective. It is likely that at least some of the statuettes of gods and goddesses are three-dimensional equivalents of deities carved or painted on the walls of other royal tombs.

Some of the funerary ideas reflected in the tomb are very old. The model boats provided the means for the King's celestial or Underworld journeys. The custom of including bows, quivers, arrows and various staves and sticks with the burial had been practised for a long time. They were usually placed inside the coffin but in Tutankhamun's tomb they were found throughout the rooms. Throwing sticks, some of them snake-shaped, belong to one of the oldest themes of tomb decoration, that of hunting birds in papyrus marshes, an activity endowed with the symbolic meaning of the pharaoh suppressing the forces of nature. A similar symbolism is conveyed by the statues of the King standing in a papyrus canoe and casting a harpoon, probably at a hippopotamus. A wooden head of Tutankhamun

THE "MAGICAL FIGURES"

There were four niches with magical figures protecting the burial in the walls of the Burial Chamber. East wall: Osiris. North wall: human figure. South wall: djed ("stability") pillar. West wall: Anubis jackal.

Anubis jackal in the West wall

Human Figure in the North wall

emerging from a lotus is the archetypal image of resurrection; the lotus which suddenly bursts open above the surface of the water is an obvious invitation for such a comparison.

Food, drink and other necessities had been tabulated in offering lists from the earliest times. In Tutankhamun's tomb they are represented by wooden containers with food, pottery jars with wine, and baskets of nuts, fruits and vegetables. There are boxes with clothing and sandals or with rolls of linen. Stone, faience and glass vessels, some of them of unusually elaborate forms, contained oils and unguents. Other vessels, as well as

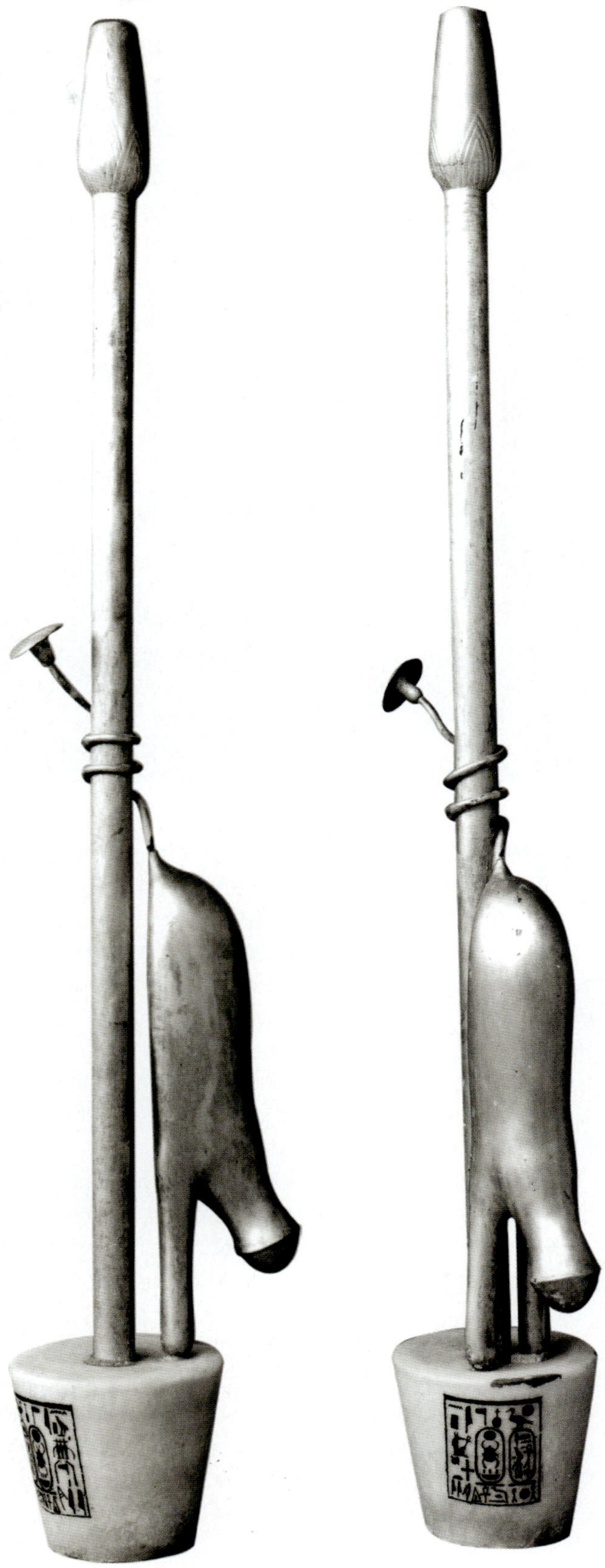

Right: Two emblems representing animal skins suspended on a pole by the tails. The inscriptions link them to the necropolis god Anubis. They were found in the Burial Chamber.

Opposite: A sleeved linen robe, with thicker fabric and needlework ornament attached to it, was found in a box in the Annexe.

367
J

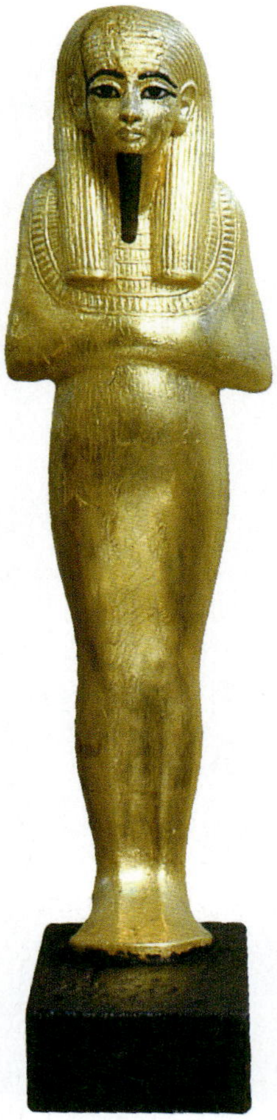

THE SHABTIS

Shabti figures and their implements (hoes, picks and baskets on yokes) are connected with ideas concerning the kingdom of Osiris. This god was the ruler of the Underworld into whose realm one hoped to be admitted after death. There was the possibility that Osiris might call upon his subjects, including the deceased king, to work in the fields or perform other menial tasks. To be prepared for such an eventuality, Tutankhamun's tomb was provided with shabtis, figures which would act as the King's substitutes to answer the call. There was one shabti for every day of the year and an overseer shabti for each ten-day week and a 30-day month.

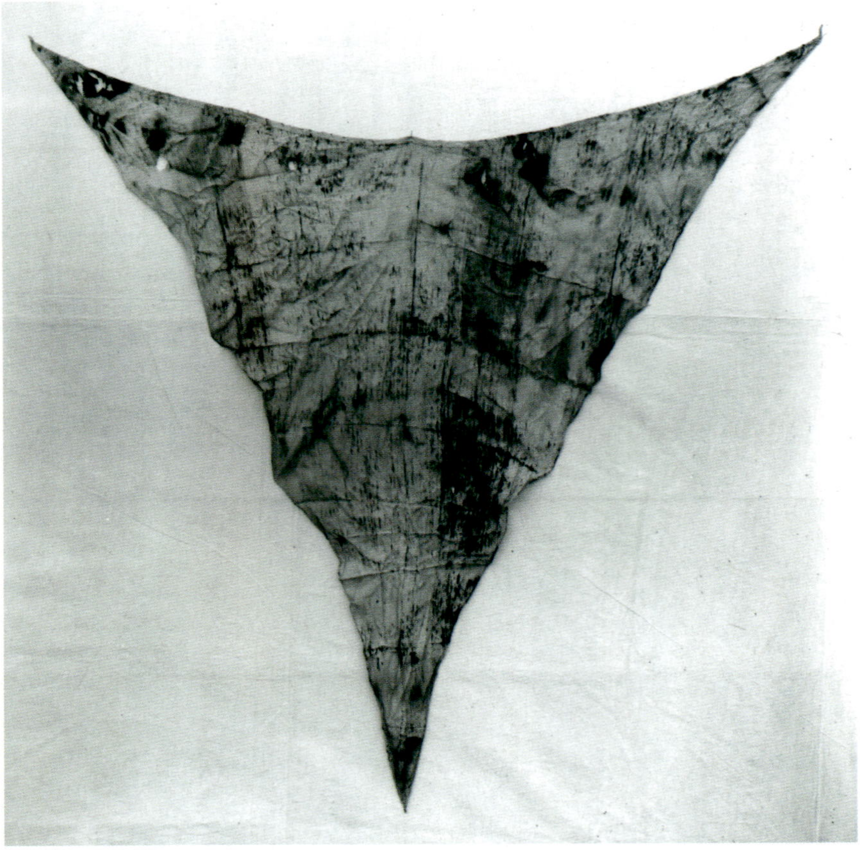

so-called kohl-tubes (tubular containers), held kohl (eye paint). There are boxes, and probably also bags, with lumps of resin and balls of incense, and shells with various pigments. Also rods of glass material were found although these are not included in early offering lists because the large-scale manufacture of glass only appeared around 1500 bc. Some basic items of furniture, for example beds and head-rests, might also be included in this category of objects.

Model implements, such as a wooden adze, are probably connected with the "opening the mouth" ceremony and faience vases and ewers of the type used for ritual libation were also found. Sistra (rattles) were used to make a sound which was thought to be pleasant to the gods. Oil-lamps, some of them made of alabaster and of complex forms, candlesticks and a reed torch on a sun-dried brick also belong to the category of ritual objects.

Shabti figures are connected with beliefs about the god Osiris as ruler of the Underworld. Also belonging to the Osiris myth was a box containing a wooden frame in the form of this god. It was filled with river silt and cereal grains and their germination symbolized his annual resurrection. A model granary and quern (grinding stone) with a grinder, as well as imitation sickles, refer to the tasks the King might be called upon to perform in the kingdom of Osiris.

The function of the three massive couches (cow-, hippopotamus-, and lion-headed), specially made for the tomb, is uncertain. The same is true of several rather enigmatic finds, such as the wooden goose covered with black resin, the wooden cow's head on a pedestal and the statues of Tutankhamun carried on the back of a leopard.

A large variety of amulets and some of the items of jewellery had a similarly protective function.

Opposite, above: Wooden gilded statues of the god Imsety, associated with mummified viscera, and of the lion-headed goddess Sakhmet. The latter was wrapped in a piece of linen, inscribed with the name of the Aten, and had a wreath of flowers around the neck.

Opposite, below: Two of Tutankhamun's wooden shabtis.

Above: A linen loin-cloth made of two pieces with a seam down the centre, c.91 cm (35.8 in) wide. It was found in an ornamental box in the Antechamber.

MAINTAINING TUTANKHAMUN'S ROYAL STATUS IN THE AFTERLIFE

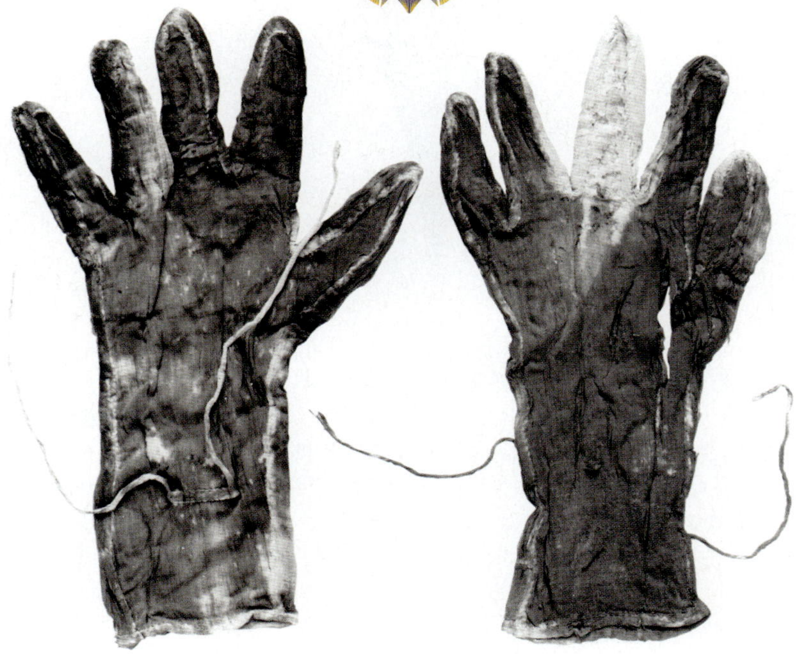

To have his mummified body recognised as that of a king was essential for Tutankhamun's admittance into the world he was going to inhabit in the afterlife. It was also important for his subjects because it guaranteed that the funerary arrangements made for them during the King's reign would be respected.

Above: Linen gloves, found in a box in the Antechamber.
Opposite, above: Mace and Lucas working on the body of one of the chariots.
Opposite, below: Parts of dismantled chariots that were found in the Antechamber.

143
121
116
120
112
114
113
115
118
119
123

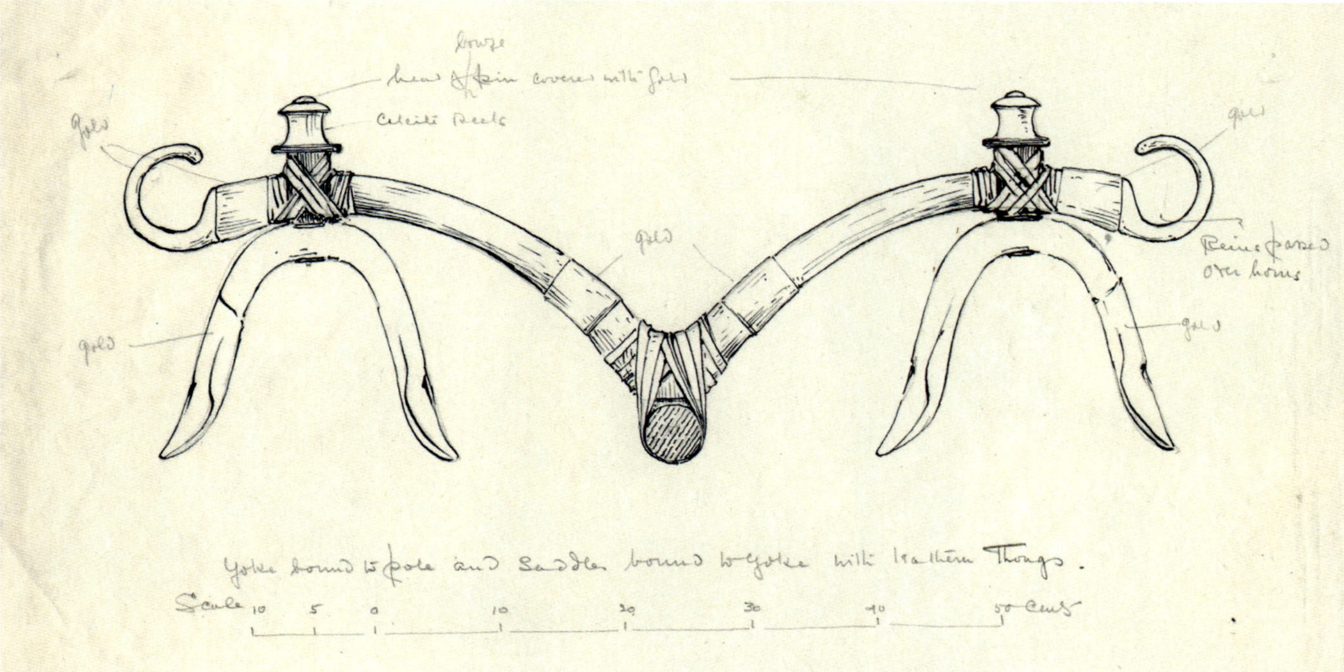

Tutankhamun is identified as a king by the location of his tomb and by the opulence of the burial (eg the gold coffins and mask) and of the funerary equipment. Other identifiers are the inscriptions on the sarcophagus, coffins and other objects in the tomb, and the inclusion of items of the King's regalia. Among these are the diadem, vulture and cobra insignia of the headdress, the sceptre (crook) and flagellum (flail), the ceremonial bull's tail, jewellery and daggers. Even Tutankhamun's shabtis, the figurines which were to act as the King's deputies should he be called to take part in public works in the Underworld, look unmistakably royal.

More sceptres, indications of royalty or divinity, were found in boxes, together with the King's ceremonial robes, including corselets and several leopard skin cloaks, sandals and many additional items of jewellery (earrings, collars, necklaces, pectorals, armlets, rings, etc). Some of the sticks also belong to these objects as well as maces, fans, horse-hair fly-whisks, bronze scimitars (sickle swords) and a leather cuirass. A visual expression of some of the royal obligations, especially the duty to subjugate Egypt's external enemies, is found on objects such as the painted box, footstools, sticks and chariots.

Judging by the differences in their decoration, the purpose of the royal chariots seems to have varied from ceremonial occasions to hunting. There were also horse harnesses, charioteer's gloves, whip handles and archer's gauntlets. Silver trumpets probably also belong to this category. Most of these objects were probably used in Tutankhamun's lifetime but

THE CHARIOTS

The chariot was introduced to Egypt around 1650 BC from Western Asia. It was used for two main purposes: as a fighting vehicle for waging war and as a means of transport for privileged sections of society. Both of these were reasons for placing chariots into the tomb. Six chariots were found in Tutankhamun's tomb (four in the Antechamber and two in the Treasury), together with many elements of harness. The chariots were dismantled and some parts, such as axles, were cut up to get them into the tomb. They were mainly made from different kinds of wood, leather, skins and bronze. Three of the chariots were sumptuously decorated in gold foil over gesso, with other materials used for inlays.

Above and opposite: Howard Carter's reconstruction of a yoke for two horses and his drawing of a horse in the yoke.

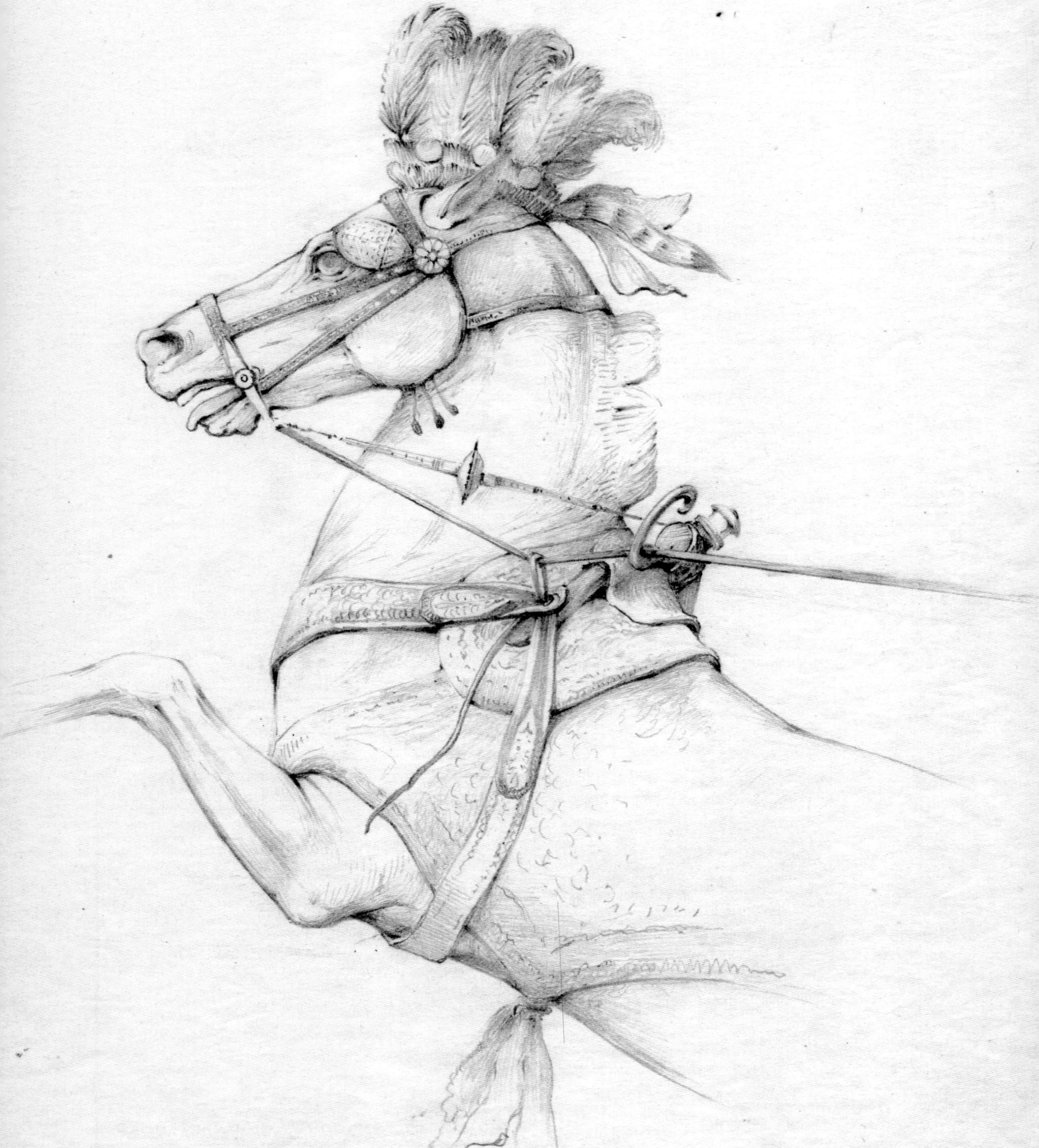

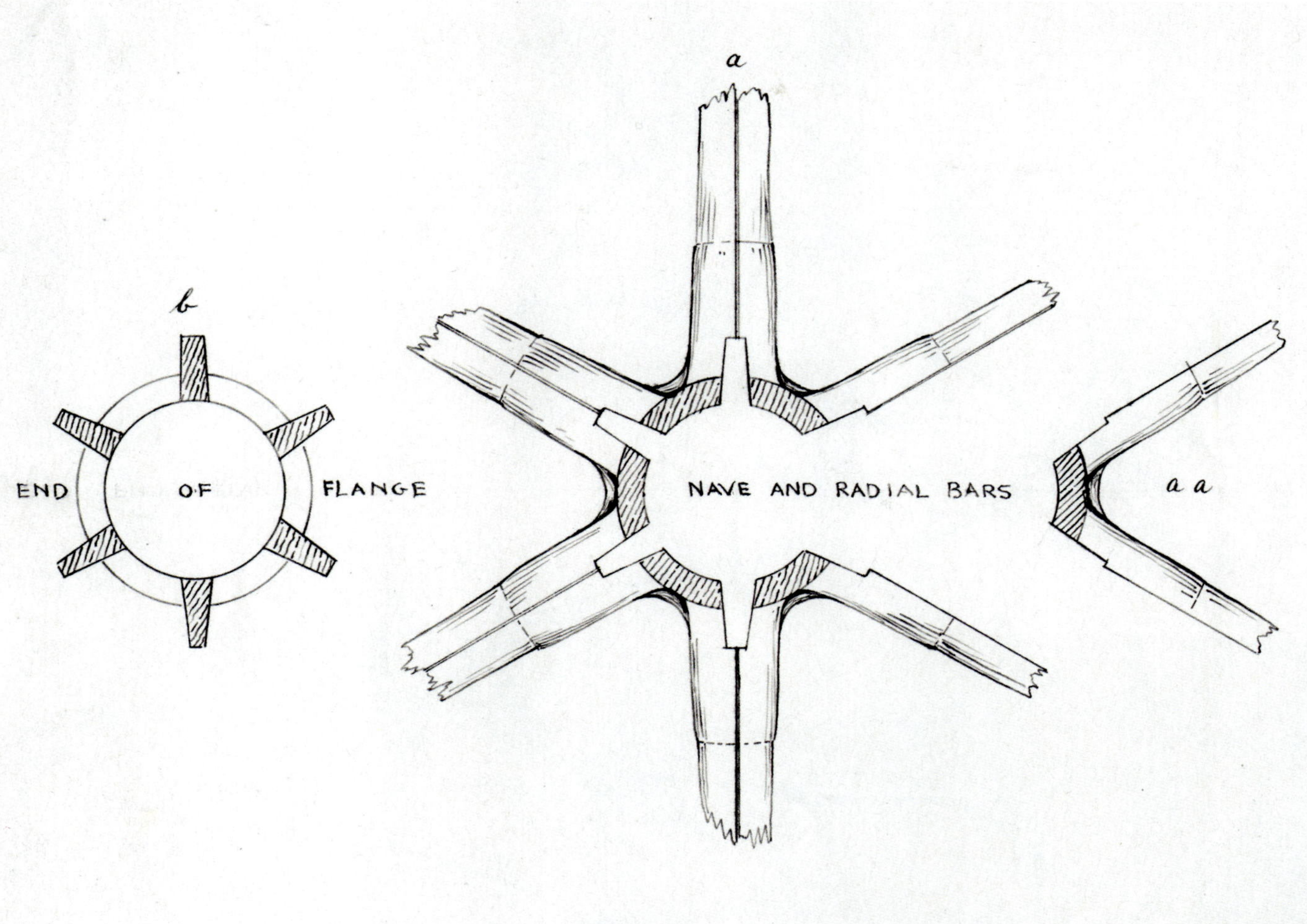

others, such as the ornamental shields, were specially made for the tomb. Less obviously royal but among items at the disposal of a king were mirrors (only their cases were found, the actual mirrors may have been removed by robbers), bronze razors and writing equipment.

Black shrine-shaped boxes on sledges with statuettes of deities may be associated with royal ceremonies in which they represented the country's districts. But many of the deities are relatively obscure and we would search in vain for some of Egypt's main gods. It is possible that these statuettes belong to the sphere of afterlife beliefs.

Above: Carter's drawings of one of the chariot wheels.

Opposite: The gold mask, probably the best-known item from Tutankhamun's tomb.

THE GOLD MASK

The purpose of the gold mask, perhaps the best known item found in the tomb, was to provide extra protection for the most important part of the King's body, his head and face, and also to make Tutankhamun immediately recognisable as a pharaoh. It is made of gold inlaid with a variety of stones (lapis lazuli, calcite, carnelian, felspar, quartz and obsidian) and coloured glass, and is 54 cm (21.25 in) high and 39.3 cm (15.5 in) wide. The text on the shoulders and back of the mask is incised and filled with white paint.

SERIES
~~BADGE~~

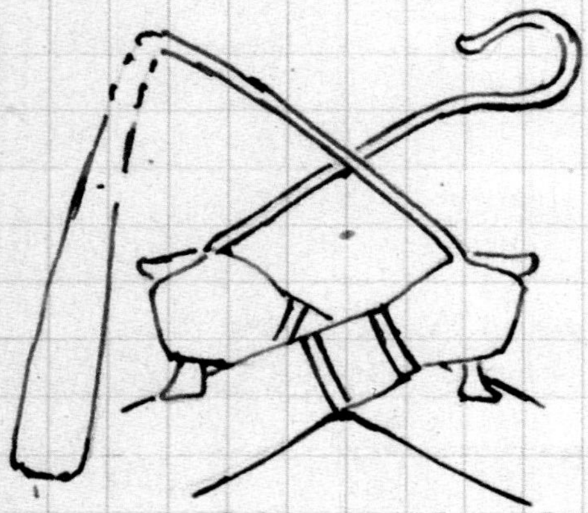

(Includes special large figures)

	SEQ. No ~~SERIES~~	MATERIAL	NO.	PROVENANCE
✓	110	Wood, Carved	1	Antechamber =
✓	318, A.	" "	1	Treasury
✓	318, B.	" "	1	"
✓	318, C.	" "	1	"
	322, A.	Quartzite	1	"
	322, B.	"	3	"
	322, E.	"	2	"
	322, G.	Granite	2	"
✓	325, A.	Wood, Carved	1	"
✓	325, B.	" "	1	"
✓	326, A.	" "	1	"
	329, A.	Quartzite	4	"
	329, E.	"	3	"
	329, H.	"	4	"
✓	330, A.	Wood, Gesso-Gilt.	1	"
✓	330, B.	" " "	1	"
✓	330, C.	" " "	1	"
✓	330, D.	" " "	1	"
✓	330, E.	" " "	1	"
✓	330, F.	" " "	1	"
✓	330, G.	" " "	1	"
✓	330, H.	" " "	1	"
✓	330, I.	Wood, Carved	1	"
✓	330, J.	" "	1	"
✓	330, K.	" "	1	"
	330, L.	Limestone.	2	"
	330, N.	"	1	" =
	337, A.	Quartzite	5	Annexe
	337, B.	"	2	"
	337, C.	"	3	"
✓	458 -	Wood Gesso-Gilt	1	"
✓	496, A	" " "	1	"
	514. A	Quartzite	4	"
	514. B	"	3	"
	514. C.	"	2	"
	514. D.	"	1	"
✓	601 -	Wood Carved	1	"
	605. D.	Quartzite	2	"
	605. E.	"	2	"
	605. G	"	4	"
✓	620 - (113)	Wood Carved	1	" =

Opposite: Pages from Howard Carter's list of shabtis.

Right: Two daggers, one of them with an iron blade, and their ornamental sheaths. Both were found on the King's mummy.

MEMENTOES OF THIS WORLD

There is little doubt that many objects found in the tomb were specially made to accompany the King into the afterlife. Tutankhamun's death was almost certainly unexpected and the pressure on the funerary workshops to provide such items at short notice was enormous. This may account for re-use or modification of some objects (e.g. the sarcophagus), perhaps originally intended for other owners. It may also explain the inclusion of items that did not reflect contemporary beliefs at the time of Tutankhamun's death and that look more like mementoes of the King's childhood.

Opposite: A close up of the back of the highly decorative chair ("throne") that was found in the Antechamber. It shows a scene of Tutankhamun being anointed by Queen Ankhesenamun.

Above left: A solid gold statuette, probably representing Amenhotep III.

Above right: The third (in a set of four) small coffin-shaped container, found in the Treasury, held another tiny coffin inscribed with the names of Queen Teye and contained a lock of plaited hair of auburn colour.

Several pieces of furniture belong to this category. There is a small ebony chair that was clearly made for a child and the reason for its inclusion may have been purely sentimental. Two of the highly decorative chairs, often called thrones, display elements of religious beliefs of the Amarna period featuring the Aten, the sun disc. Religious beliefs that centred on the Aten (the sun disc) were at the root of Akhenaten's religious reforms, but had been abandoned by the end of Tutankhamun's reign. Some of the cartouches with the King's name were brought up to date and changed from Tutankhaten ("The Living Image of the Aten") to Tutankhamun ("The Living Image of the God Amun"), but others were left untouched.

This indicates that the furniture must have been manufactured much earlier. The changes might have been made only when a shortage of funerary equipment led to their incorporation in the tomb. But the alterations were superficial and it is quite remarkable that beliefs that represented complete negation of the traditional religion were not regarded as being harmful to Tutankhamun's afterlife.

The explanation of other objects remains elusive, for example small limestone and glass statuettes, which may represent Akhenaten. One would like to regard them as genuine mementoes. A disturbingly modern idea, although we do not fully grasp its implications, seems inherent in a set of four small anthropoid coffins found in the Treasury. The innermost is inscribed with the name of Queen Teye, the chief wife of Amenhotep III (and so Tutankhamun's grandmother). It contains a lock of plaited hair. In the same group of material there is a small solid gold statuette, which may represent Amenhotep III himself.

The purpose of the so-called mannequin figure is uncertain, but it may have been practical rather than religious. Another puzzling piece is a tiny bronze figure of a dog found in the Annexe that does not appear to have any religious significance.

THE THRONE

The present appearance of this armchair (sometimes called a "golden throne") is somewhat misleading. Originally, there were openwork designs symbolising the union of Upper and Lower Egypt in the spaces between the legs and the struts and it must have looked heavier. The chair is made of wood covered with sheet gold and inlaid in silver, semiprecious stones, calcite, faience and glass; the feet have bronze shoes. The armrests are in the form of winged serpents. There are two lion's heads at the front of the seat and the legs terminate in lion's paws. The back support has a scene of Tutankhamun being anointed by his wife Ankhesenamun. The Aten, the main religious symbol of Akhenaten's reign, radiates its rays terminated in human hands above the couple. The names in the cartouches next to Tutankhamun and Ankhesenamun were altered from the earlier forms that contained the name of the Aten; the names on the rear of the back were left unchanged. Since the King changed his name very early in his reign, the scene shows him at the age of not more than about 10 or 11.

THE DUCK-HEAD CHAIR

The design of this chair (sometimes called a "ceremonial throne") is unusual and quite witty: it imitates another type of furniture, but does not function as such. It is made of ebony and ivory covered with gold foil and inlays. The form is that of an open folding stool ("faldstool") with an additional slightly sloping back support, which transforms it into a chair. Its legs terminate in duck heads and the seat, although also made of wood and therefore solid, is inlaid to resemble animal skin. The inscriptions on the chair refer to the King as Tutankhaten and this dates it to the beginning of the reign, before the change of the name took place.

Opposite: The highly decorative chair ("throne") that was found in the Antechamber.

Below, left: The King's early form of his name, Tutankhaten, is in the cartouches (ornamental frames) flanking the goddess Nekhbet, shown as a vulture. The chair comes from the Annexe.

Below: The "mannequin", a wooden bust of the King, was of uncertain purpose and was found in the Antechamber.

KING TUTANKHAMUN

Tutankhamun is sometimes described as an unimportant pharaoh who is famous only because his tomb with its fabulous treasures has been found largely intact. This is hardly a fair assessment. Tutankhamun was at the helm of Egypt, even though acting on advice, during one of the most complex times in its history. The country was regressing into orthodoxy, after two turbulent decades of the Amarna period, and the reign must be seen as a stepping stone towards a new and exciting era dominated by the Ramessids.

Above: A statue showing Tutankhamun (centre) between the god Amun (right) and the goddess Mut (left), found at Karnak. Tutankhamun is represented as the junior member of the triad.

Opposite, left: A wooden gilded statue of Tutankhamun holding a flagellum (flail) and a long crooked staff. It was found in the Treasury.

Below, right: Ankhesenamun arranges jewellery round Tutankhamun's neck, shown on a wooden gilded shrine from the Antechamber.

Very little is known about Tutankhamun (who was at first called Tutankhaten) before he became king. We are not even absolutely certain who his parents were. The most logical assumption, however, is that he was the son of King Akhenaten (1353–1337 BC). However, he is never shown with his father and Queen Nefertiti. A possible explanation is that his mother was a minor royal wife, perhaps called Kiya. Not all historians agree, and suggestions have been made that he was a son of Amenhotep III (this would require a long joint rule between Amenhotep III and Akhenaten, which is

THE CULT TEMPLE

Although the location of royal tombs of New Kingdom pharaohs (1540–1069 BC) was not secret, access to the Valley of the Kings was restricted in ancient times. The rock-cut tombs were sealed and made inaccessible and there were no temples in the Valley where the cult of the deceased kings could be maintained by performing ceremonies and bringing offerings. The cult temples were built along the west bank of the Nile, at a distance of some 1.5–2.5 km (about 1–1.5 miles) from the Valley of the Kings. Tutankhamun probably had such a temple, but it almost certainly was small and has not yet been located. It may have been somewhere near the cult temple of Aye and Haremhab close to Medinet Habu.

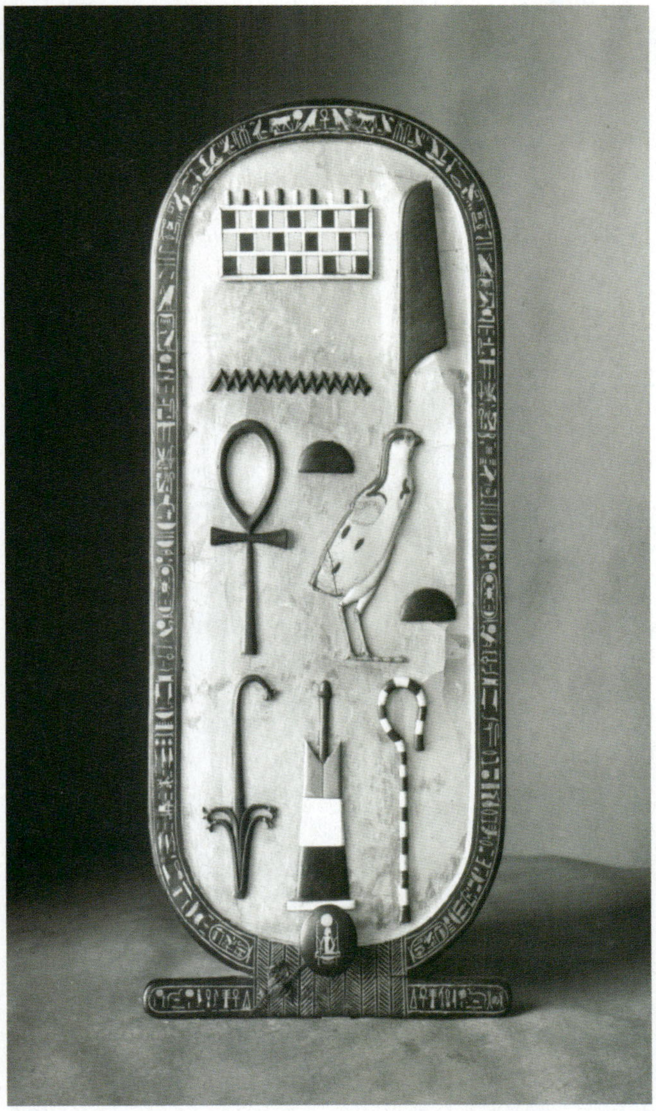

TUTANKHAMUN'S NAMES

Like other Egyptian kings, Tutankhamun had five official royal names:

The Horus name: Tut-mesut, "The image of rebirths".

The Two Ladies name: Neferhepu-segerehtaui, "One perfect of laws, who pacifies the Two Lands".

The Golden Horus name: Wetjes-khau-sehetep-netjeru, "One who has raised the crowns, the pacifier of the gods".

The King of Upper and Lower Egypt name: Nebkheprure, "The god Ra is the possessor of forms".

The Son of the God Ra name: First Tutankhaten, "The living image of the Aten", then Tutankhamun-heka-iunu-shema, "The living image of the god Amun, the ruler of Upper Egyptian On (= Thebes)".

"The King I most desired to find."

Howard Carter

unlikely) or a son of one of the many daughters of Amenhotep III, but the argument is not fully convincing.

Tutankhamun's predecessor was King Smenkhkare (1338–1336 BC),a figure who was even more enigmatic than Tutankhamun himself (even Smenkhkare's gender has been queried). The two were almost certainly related, but it is not clear how. Tutankhamun's mummy shows that he died at the age of about 19, and the highest date of the reign, recorded on a wine jar found in his tomb, is his tenth year. This means that he must have been about nine at his accession.

As Tutankhaten, the King at first resided at Akhetaten (El-Amarna). But in less than two years he moved his residence to the old capital, Mennufer (Memphis). Senior courtiers accompanied him and the city of Akhetaten was abandoned. The King changed his name to Tutankhamun and so renounced the Aten and indicated his return to the old gods by replacing it with Amun instead.

Tutankhamun's queen, the only one we know of, was Ankhesenpaten, the third daughter of Akhenaten and Nefertiti and a few years older than he. She followed her husband's example and replaced the Aten in her name by Amun, and so became Ankhesenamun. It seems that at Tutankhamun's death there were no surviving offspring; their two daughters were stillborn and were buried with him in his tomb.

The reign of Tutankhamun witnessed a gradual return to orthodoxy in all areas, especially religion. But there is no evidence that this was carried out in a violent way. The memory of the Aten was not actively persecuted and the careers of many officials who had been closely connected with the Amarna regime continued seemingly little affected. The fortunes of temples of the traditional gods, especially those of Amun, were restored: their religious importance was reinstated, their property was returned and their buildings repaired and reconstructed. New building activities, however, were limited.

The precise cause of Tutankhamun's death remains uncertain, but when he died the Thutmosid line of kings, which had begun more than 200 years earlier, died with him. His successor, Aye, was not of royal blood.

Opposite: A wooden box in the form of a cartouche (an ornamental frame) containing the name of Tutankhamun. The hieroghlyphs are made of ivory and ebony on a gold background.

Above, left: Tutankhamun pours a libation onto Ankhesenamun's hand, depicted on a gilded shrine.

Above, right: Ankhesenamun holding Tutankhamun's arm. This is shown on a gilded shrine.

AND 97 YEARS LATER...

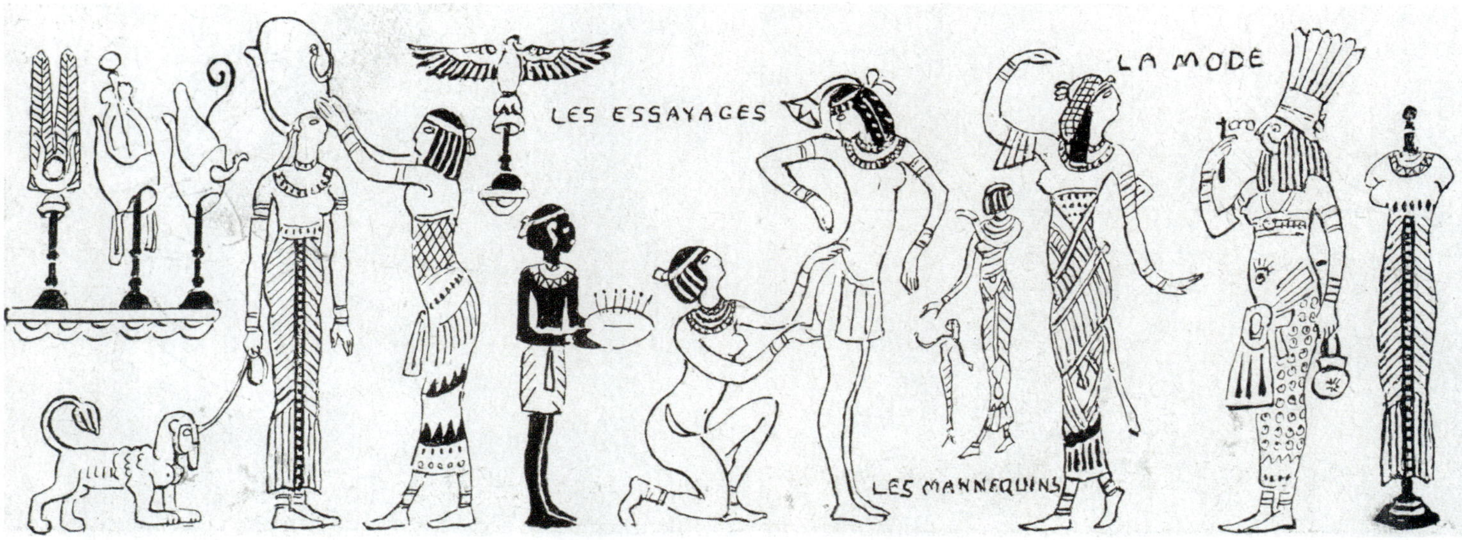

The decade during which Howard Carter and his colleagues worked in the tomb of Tutankhamun was full of excitement, but not all of it was archaeological. There were tensions within the team, difficulties in dealing with the Egyptian Government, with the Antiquities Service, and a strained relationship with the Press. Sometimes Carter himself may have been at fault, but the mere fact that he was able to withstand all this pressure and complete the recording of the tomb is a huge achievement for which he must be admired.

Above: Nothing new under the sun! Female fashion satirized by comparison with ancient Egypt in the aftermath of the discovery of Tutankhamun's tomb. This illustration, by H Avelot, appeared in La Vie Parisienne, on 10 March 1923.

Opposite: Crowds queuing patiently for admission to the 1972 Tutankhamun exhibition at the British Museum in London.

The tomb of Tutankhamun was discovered almost one hundred years ago. The objects, with the exception of the mummy, the sarcophagus and one coffin, which are still in the tomb, and the foetuses, botanical specimens and a few other items, which may or may not have originated from the tomb, are in the Egyptian Museum in Cairo. Many of them are on display and are admired by thousands of visitors every day. Pictures of Tutankhamun's objects have been reproduced in countless books and articles and many items have toured the world as part of exhibitions. Tutankhamun's gold mask is one of the most widely recognizable icons of our times. The discovery has inspired many young people to take up archaeology or Egyptology. It has influenced popular culture in the widest sense, including architecture, design, fashion, literature, film and television.

Because the finds have not yet been fully published, any evaluation of the tomb's contribution to our knowledge of ancient Egypt can, at present, be only provisional. But nevertheless, it is instructive to consider it. If we disregard the tomb's emotional appeal, which areas of Egyptology have been significantly advanced by the discovery of the tomb? Not the Egyptian language. The tomb contains no papyri and the texts on objects found in the tomb are fairly unexceptional. Not Egyptian history. We are better informed about the length of Tutankhamun's reign and we know more about the survival of Amarna elements in the post-Amarna age, but the tomb contained no truly historical documents. A considered and well-informed assessment of the tomb's contribution to religious and funerary customs is still lacking. The history of art is one of the least advanced areas of Egyptology and any general statement concerning this aspect would be premature. As for mummification, the King's mummy and the foetuses of his children yield little new information.

The main contribution of the tomb may, therefore, be rather unexpected. Firstly, we have an almost perfectly preserved corpus of first-class contemporary material from the end of the 18th dynasty, an archaeologist's dream. Secondly, its importance need not lie in traditional Egyptological scholarship, but in the history of technology. Much of what we know about artefacts derives mainly

The hundreds of tourists witness
the removal of the Royal Cou
Couch, embellished with gold.

Removal of one side of the Royal Couch
Lord Carnavon & his daughter
Lady Evelyn Herbert following.

Opposite: Pages from an album of pictures taken by the paparazzi outside the tomb in 1923.

Right: Tourists watching the removal of objects from the tomb into the "laboratory" (the tomb of Sety II).

Below: The discovery of the tomb of Tutankhamun made people all over the world aware of ancient Egypt. This was soon exploited by the advertising industry.

CARTER AFTER TUTANKHAMUN

The concession for work in the Valley of the Kings, originally given to Lord Carnarvon and retained by his widow after his death, expired in October 1929. The recording of Tutankhamun's tomb had, by then, been finished, although the transport of the massive shrines from the Burial Chamber to Cairo and their installation in the Museum took another three years. The last Tutankhamun season came to a close in February 1932. Carter's remaining years were spent quietly; partly in England, partly in Egypt in his house at Elwet el-Diban that had been his base during the work in the tomb. He was physically and mentally exhausted and took no further part in any excavations. The third volume of *The Tomb of Tut-Ankh-Amen* was published in 1933. In Britain, Carter had few friends among Egyptologists and received no official honour. In his last years he suffered from ill health and died on 2 March 1939.

from representations or rather poorly preserved specimens, with all the drawbacks this carries. But the tomb of Tutankhamun is a treasure trove of actual and mostly well-preserved objects. There is an enormous difference between an image of an object and the object itself, because only the latter can actually be studied for the details of design, manufacture and the materials used to construct it. The tomb of Tutankhamun shows us how the Egyptians made furniture, jewellery, textiles, basketry, and countless other objects found in it.

The last word about this tomb and its contents certainly has not been said. But one thing is certain. There is nothing like this moving and magnificent collection of ancient objects from anywhere else in the world.

Left: An extract from a tourist souvenir album of a trip to Egypt in 1923. It includes a visit to the recently discovered tomb of Tutankhamun.

Opposite: An extract from the Illustrated London News, 16 December 1922.

PUBLICATION

To date, only a relatively small number of the objects, probably less than 20 per cent, have been published in a way that modern Egyptology would expect. There are complex reasons for this state of affairs: the sheer size of the discovery, Carter's determination to publish the material himself, his deteriorating health and his premature death, and the fact that many of the objects are made of precious metal, which makes access to them more difficult. Only the following categories of objects have so far been systematically analysed and published in detail: the sarcophagus, bows, human remains, chariots, musical instruments, game boxes, model boats, the small golden shrine, stone vessels, pottery and sealings, the "painted box" and the shrines. A handful of individual items have also been studied. Hieroglyphic and hieratic inscriptions from all the objects have been completely published, although only the latter with translations and commentaries.

THE ILLUSTRATED LONDON NEWS

REGISTERED AS A NEWSPAPER FOR TRANSMISSION IN THE UNITED KINGDOM AND TO CANADA AND NEWFOUNDLAND BY MAGAZINE POST.

SATURDAY, DECEMBER 16, 1922.

WHAT THE GREAT "FIND" IN EGYPT MAY BRING: A 3000-YEAR-OLD PHARAOH "COMING FORTH INTO THE DAY," WITH THE CONTEMPORARY GARLANDS, WHICH ADORNED HIS MUMMY.

"The old Egyptians," writes Dr. H. R. Hall, of the British Museum, "prayed ever that they, who 'loved life and hated death,' might not remain for ever in the night of death, but might 'come forth into the day,' and live still as they had on earth. The name of the funerary chapters, the prayers and spells which we call the 'Book of the Dead,' buried with them to ensure their welfare in the next world, was 'The Book of Coming forth into the Day.' . . . The latest discovery of an ancient royal sepulchre, that of King Tutankhamen, by Lord Carnarvon and Mr. Howard Carter, is perhaps the greatest of all. The present writer remembers how twenty years ago he assisted at the coming forth into the day of a long-dead Egyptian king. He came forth for the very modern purpose of being photographed, borne on the shoulders of four stalwart descendants of his subjects, while others lighted his progress with torches. Official authority, in the person of the Inspector-General of Antiquities, was there to supervise and take the photograph: his humble subordinate, the native *ghafir*, or watchman of the tombs, stood by with staff in hand and brassard on arm; the archæologist from a distant museum looked on. The photographing completed, the dead king was borne back again to his sarcophagus, where he now sleeps still surrounded by the garlands with which his mummy was adorned more than three thousand years ago."

DRAWN BY OUR SPECIAL ARTIST, A. FORESTIER, FROM INFORMATION SUPPLIED BY DR. H. R. HALL, OF THE BRITISH MUSEUM.

PICTURE CREDITS

The publishers would like to thank the following sources for their kind permission to reproduce the pictures in this book.

AKG London: 91, /Andrea Jemolo: 19, Erich Lessing: 54
BILDARCHIV PREUBISCLHER KULTURB: /Agyptisches Museum und Papyrussammlung, Staatliche Museen zu Berlin/Jurgen Liepe: 12 TR
BRITISH MUSEUM: 27L, 43
CORBIS IMAGES: /Chris Lisle: 35 T, /Roger Wood: 83 T
DURHAMM ORIENTAL MUSEUM: 33 B
GETTY IMAGES: /Fox Photos: 141, /Ethan Miller: 135 R, / Robert Harding: 131, /The Bridgeman Art Library: 29, 112 BR
GRIFFITH INSTITUTE: 21 B, 25, 27 R, 32, 33 TR, 34, 36, 37, 38 BR, 37 T, 37 B, 38, 39, 39 B, 40, 41, 42 L, 42 R, 44 R, 44 L, 45 T, 45 BR, 55 BL, 46, 47, 48 BL, 48 BR, 49, 50, 51, 52, 53 L, 53 R, 54-55, 57 T, 57 BL, 57 BR, 58, 59, 60, 61, 62 B, 63, 64, 65 TL, 65 TR, 65 BR, 65 BL, 66 BR, 66 BL, 68, 69, 70, 71 B, 71 T, 72, 73, 74, 78 T, 78 TC, 78 TR, 78 B, 79 T, 79 BL, 79 T, 79 BR, 80, 81, 82 R, 83B, 84, 85, 86, 87 TR, 87 BR, 87 TL, 90, 92, 93, 94, 95, 96, 97, 98, 99, 100, 101, 102, 103 T, 104, 105, 106, 107 TR, 107 TL, 107 BL, 108 L, 111 B, 111 T, 112 LC, 112 BL, 115, 116 T, 117 BR, 119 B, 119 T, 120 R, 120 TL, 121, 123, 124, 125 T, 125 R, 126, 127, 129, 130, 133 R, 133 L, 138, 139 R, 142, 143 T, 144.
ILLUSTRATED LONDON NEWS: 145
MARY EVANS PICTURE LIBRARY: 140
METROPOLITAN MUSEUM OF ART: 76
DR R. PARKINSON: 62 T
PHOTOS 14: 17, 18, 27 B, /Jean Guichard: 8, 13 L, 15, /Oronoz: 22 T
PICTURE DESK: /Art Archive/Egyptian Museum Cairo: 125 BL, / Art Archive/Egyptian Museum Cairo/Dagli Orti: 13R, 16, 82 L, 122 T, 132, 135 L, /Art Archive/Luxor Museum Egypt/Dagli Orti: 117 BL, 122 B, /Art Archive/Musee Du Louvre Paris/Dagli Orti: 30, /Art Archive/Dagli Orti: 26.
REX FEATURES: /Action Press: 137 L, /Sipa Press: 103 B.
SCIENCE PHOTO LIBRARY: /Space Imaging Europe: 9
THE ADVERTISING ARCHIVE: 143 B
THE BRIDGEMAN ART LIBRARY: /Egypian Museum Cairo: 110, /Egyptian Museum Cairo: 75, 113, 116 B, 117 TR, 118, 134, / Egyptian Museum Cairo/Boltin Picture Library: 114, 129, 137 R, 139 L, /Royal Society London: 28 T
TOPHAM PICTUREPOINT: 109 BR, 136, /British Museum London: 31, /Spectrum Colour Library: 88
WERNER FORMAN ARCHIVE: 11, 14, /British Museum London: 21, /Egyptian Museum Berlin: 23, /Egyptian Museum Cairo: 20, 24, 28 B, /El-Minya Museum: 22 B, /E. Strouhal: 10, 89 L, 89 R

Every effort has been made to acknowledge correctly and contact the source and/or copyright holder of each picture and Future Publishing Limited apologises for any unintentional errors or omissions which will be corrected in future editions of this book.